Cyril Fletcher
Planning The Small Garden

Cyril Fletcher

Planning Th

First published 1981
© copyright Cyril Fletcher 1981
ISBN 0 00 410405 6
Printed and bound in Spain
by Graficromo, S.A.–Córdoba

mall Garden

Collins

To Betty,
my darling wife, who has shared
and inspired many gardens
I have lovingly created for her

Foreword

by F. C. Nutbeam, M.V.O., F.N.V.S.
recently retired Head Gardener at Buckingham Palace

I have spent many hours and had much pleasure in reading the manuscript and studying the garden designs in this book and have no doubt of its potential value both to the keen amateur and the humble beginner.

The author is writing with a serious purpose in mind—to describe and display with a very comprehensive list of trees, shrubs and plants some sound advice and nicely executed plans—very useful material for those who, perhaps for the first time in their lives, find themselves the proud possessors of a piece of land, wondering what to do and where to begin.

Your garden may be a bare plot, a site full of builders' rubble, a piece of woodland, or if you are extremely lucky a sadly neglected garden of past glory. You may as some do concrete it over. Hopefully you may wish for a thing of beauty —the garden of your dreams—either to equal or surpass your neighbours' or to give pleasure and delight to your friends and family.

After a lifetime as a professional, maintaining and making gardens for other people, and in retirement planning and constructing one for myself for pleasure and profit, I know only too well that this is only hard and time-consuming work —there are short cuts but not many. Over the years in my travels round the country judging I have seen the most unlikely and the most wonderful creations contrived by the oddest of people in the oddest of places—house-tops in central London, over tottering garage roofs, one over a coffin-maker's shop, dark basement areas. Nothing seems impossible if the owner has that rare gift to create beauty.

The author of this book is better known to millions of radio listeners and television viewers as the 'Odd Oder' (Cyril to all his friends), well known on ATV for his *Gardening Today* programme with Bob Price (on which I had the good fortune to be one of their first guests) and to Londoners for his weekly gardening chat and monthly 'phone-in' on Capital Radio. It has been for Capital Radio that for the last few years he has designed and shown those superb small gardens at the Chelsea Flower Show that have aroused much interest and won medals for him on each occasion.

These are by no means the only incursions Cyril Fletcher has made into the gardening world. He and his dear wife Betty, two of the most practical, knowledgeable and kindly people I know, with many pursuits and interests, have been designing and making gardens of their own for all of their married life.

Contents

Introduction

It is always a daunting prospect for a writer to sit down and look at a blank piece of paper and to know that his living depends on what will eventually fill the page. It must be similarly daunting for the new owner of a house to look out at his patch of garden, saying to himself 'How do I start?' He finds the prospect additionally worrying because he knows that this piece of land is possibly one of his most valuable possessions (apart from his wife!). He therefore must not spoil it—or waste it—but must make the very best use of it: for his soul and his stomach!

He will also want to garden this piece of land himself. A useful definition of a 'small garden' is one big enough or small enough to be cared for by one person in his spare time. It is the amount of spare time he must be especially honest about, because the time he can spend on this garden will in many ways dictate its design.

At the back of this book, starting on page 94, you will find fifteen plans which are designed to cope with both the shape and plot you are landed with and the amount of time you can spend cherishing it.

Planning a new garden is an exciting prospect—I'll never forget owning my first garden, when I was young and enthusiastic and nothing could have stopped me from jumping up and down in it, shouting 'Mine! All mine!' It was my piece of England and I was going to enjoy every square inch of it!

But because you are enthusiastic I beg of you, dear Reader, do not *rush* at this garden. There are two reasons for studied tranquility. One is, if you do things too quickly, without a lot of thought and reason, more than likely you will have to undo some of your first hard work and do it again; and secondly, if you dash at it with all your energy—especially if you are not used to manual labour, you will tire yourself out and give yourself not only awful aches and pains but a distaste for the whole procedure before you have even begun.

Your garden is going to be not only an extension of your home, but of your personality. If you are artistic and not very practical then it will be a lovely shambles of a garden. If you are very practical and not at all artistic, then you will have regimented plants and lots of clean bare soil and plants tied clinically to sticks, as if they were hospital splints! But if you are both artistic and practical then the result will be paradise! Let us wax lyrical and say that if poetry is God's message expressed through the medium of man's pen, then the art of gardening is the painting of nature's picture by man.

Chapter
1

Count your assets

Aspects. Soil. Shape.

Please step out of your new house on to your completely bare new garden, or, if you have moved to an old house—the old garden we are about to re-design.

You must first decide on the aspect of the garden. Do you face south? Due south is where most sunshine comes from, and if your garden faces and slopes to the south as well, you are the most favoured of gardeners. If it faces and slopes south west, the next luckiest, south east, the next—and if you face due north you are the unluckiest of all. Do not despair if you do, because there are plants which will revel in this adversity, and there are many ways in which gardening expertise can mitigate your misfortune.

But should you face west, here is a little trick you will thank me for many times, if you carry it out. Arrange a theme of red and mauve and chestnut-coloured foliage together with red, orange and purple flowers. You will thank me every time the sun sets redly when all your colours will seem to have a luminosity of their own, as if they were shining back at the sun. Have some night-scented things here too, like stocks and tobacco plants, to add to the enchantment.

Light is important. It is the action of light on the leaves of a plant (photosynthesis) creating the necessary plant foods which, together with the food and moisture from the plants' roots, make it grow. Today town air is so much cleaner that plants and trees, which would never have been able to survive years ago, can now grow in the centre of a town.

You now know which way you face. Does the garden slope at all? I do hope it does, because if a garden is flat it is much

less interesting than a garden on several levels. Indeed, if it is completely flat then you will have to lower some of the garden, using the soil you take out to build up another part; making sure always to leave the topsoil on top. Never bury the topsoil as it contains more humus and nutrients than the subsoil and is therefore not only more valuable but easier to work. If you are on a steep slope you must terrace it; that is to say, make a series of gigantic steps with retaining walls to hold back the earth contained in each level. If the slope is slight, one shallow step will do, or even a slight slope.

Are there any trees? The whole appearance of a garden is enhanced by the magnificence of mature trees. You do not want many large trees in a small garden, however; but I do implore you, do not be hasty over the removal of *any* mature tree—it takes perhaps a couple of lifetimes to grow and only an hour or so with a mechanical saw to cut down and destroy all that beauty. No matter how shady it makes you, no matter how much it is going to drip on your washing, do not, at least for the first year, cut down a tree. Do not lop a great lump off it either—that way you may make the tree forever an eyesore. There are so many varieties of small trees for a small garden, you will be bewildered when I come to tell you about them in Chapter V. Some you will plant because they are quick growing, others because of their blossoms or their scent; how beautiful and how beneficent they are and, usually, how easy to grow, given that you follow faithfully a few tried and true rules.

If you have an old garden the rule is to see it right through a whole year before you remove anything—this way you will know what flowers when, and whether you like it or not. You will know what the herbaceous plants are and what bulb treasures are hiding beneath the soil. When a friend of mine moved to a new house and garden, he laboriously planted five thousand bulbs in an orchard in the late summer. In late autumn he got a local chap in to help saw up a dead apple tree. As he straightened his back the local yokel said, 'Aah! You'll like this orchard in the spring. If there's one daffodil bulb in this grass there must be ten thousand. In April it's a picture!'

Type of Soil Now, we have to find out what kind of soil you have in your garden. Whether your soil is acid or alkaline is most important, as this factor will decide the sort of plants you will be able to grow. All things considered, let's hope it is acid because an acid soil will allow you to grow many more of the worthwhile plants. If it is alkaline, this is a challenge you will meet by choosing only those plants which are happy in an alkaline soil. 'How do I find out?' you are saying, so I will tell you.

If you are a member of the Royal Horticultural Society (and all keen gardeners should be, as not only can you see the annual Chelsea Flower Show and all the other shows the RHS holds fortnightly, but you can also visit and learn from their marvellous gardens at Wisley in Surrey), they will carry out a soil test for you if you send them a suitable sample. If you are not a member you could have your soil tested by your local Agricultural Advisory Service for a small fee. The test will give you what the pH value of your soil is. The principle of the test is based on a colour change—rather like the litmus paper test we did in chemistry lessons at school. The pH scale is a measure of acidity. An acid soil has a pH value below 7. An alkaline soil has a pH value above 7. As lime is added to your soil, so its pH value will increase.

If you would rather try your hand at carrying out the soil test yourself, go to your nearest seedsman's shop or gardening centre and there buy a small kit for this purpose.

Sandy soils These are light, well aerated and easy to dig, free-draining, and warm up quickly in the spring. Unfortunately, they lose moisture quickly in hot weather. Feed the hungry brute with as much compost, peat, spent hops and farmyard manure as possible to keep the soil open.

Chalk or alkaline soils These soils are too rich in lime. They need abundant organic matter.

Stony and gravel soils These are similar in a way to sandy soils, only the granules are larger and, as it were, have become stones. Such soils are usually thin and require humus. The undersides of the stones form a reservoir of water for plants, and they also keep the soil cool.

Loamy soils This is sand and humus and clay all in a perfect blend like the best Scotch whisky. It's a joy to work. You will need manure and compost but not nearly so much as for other soils.

Clay soil This is a heavy soil which is sometimes impossible to work after rain. If your subsoil of clay goes down several feet you will have to drain it with field drains or utilize broken bricks and rubble, making a trench leading to a soakaway. For general treatment of a clay soil, drain if absolutely necessary, break up your subsoil, take away your clay and then import a good garden loam from a garden centre. Expensive yes, but it saves many a heartache and—many a rupture. If you are going to persevere with the clay you will need to burn some. A vigorous fire of wood is enclosed with clods of clay. After burning, the residue is friable (easily crumbled) and helps the texture of the remaining soil. Add ashes and humus of all kinds. Green manuring helps; green manuring is either digging in all weeds, or sowing some member of the pea family—vetches, lupins, etc.—and digging them in at the height of their lushest growth. Thompson & Morgan of Ipswich do a special green manure mixture of seeds. Compost is valuable for *all* soils. Compost all your waste material and dig it in continuously.

11

Planning The Small Garden

A good example of a mixed border at Hidcote. You could follow this for a long narrow cottage garden

A dry wall of Mucklow stone makes an attractive retaining wall for a rockery

If you move to an old garden see it through a whole year before moving anything—daffodils are often a lovely surprise!

Planning The Small Garden

Designs on your shape What is the shape of the garden? Long and narrow is the most popular, soul-destroying and, regrettably, usual shape, with identical fences on either side and across the bottom. Sometimes it is wide but short and sometimes, because the house was built on the last little bit of the estate, you have a garden shaped like the most improbable piece of a thousand-piece jigsaw puzzle. In some ways, though, you are the luckiest because this shape of garden presents such a challenge. So few gardeners realize the challenge of their long and narrow strip. You have got to split it up. You have got to use curves, circles, lozenges and ovals — even a jolly rhomboid (no, I don't know what that means either) to split up and camouflage the shape. You should not be able to see all of it at once: your eye should be led on to see what is round the corner.

Draw a plan of your garden — this is the plan for the 'country' town garden I designed for the Chelsea Flower Show (see page 118 for planting details)

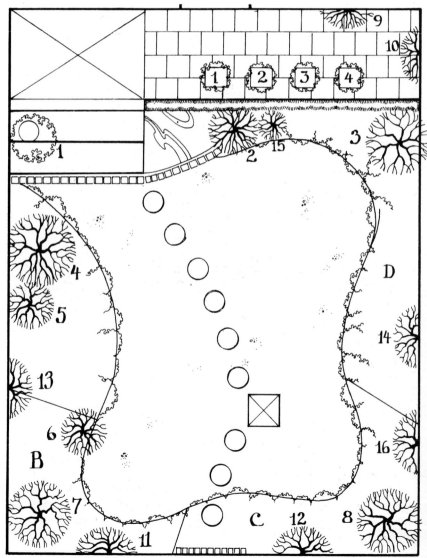

How do you make these shapes? You must first of all make a plan to scale on paper of your actual garden with all its peculiarities and idiosyncrasies and then decide roughly on the shapes you need. Shapes are sometimes dictated by a feature present in your garden, like a tree, clump of trees, pond, terrace or whatever is there, which you feel you would like to retain, or which you would like to instal if it is a new garden.

I can tell you how to plant properly, how to drain, how to plant hedges, trees and herbaceous plants. I can advise on how to construct steps, dry walls, ponds and fountains even, but I cannot decide, because of your individual site, and, indeed, because of your individual likes and dislikes, on the final collection of ingredients which will go to make your garden.

You were saying, 'How am I to achieve these various shapes?' My answer is—in many ways. You may use hedges, paths, shaped beds with shaped lawns to contain them, walls, different levels contained by small walls, ponds, walls and arched entrances, gates made of wood or wrought iron, plantings of trees and shrubs and herbaceous plants; a selection of the foregoing; or you may achieve your result by the positioning of a summerhouse or a statue or a pergola (a covered walk of stone or wooden pillars with roses and other climbing plants over it). In short, your choices are many and varied.

All I can do, therefore, is suggest to you a few different plans to help you to create satisfying shapes and forms for your garden and try to help to cure some of the problems the shape of your garden presents.

To fit in with the simplicity of modern architecture it will be necessary to think simply; to think of clean lines and geometrical shapes for the bones of the garden. Various textures, shapes and colours of the plants will give body and a welcome naturalness to offset and soften the starkness of some of the modern shapes and materials. Don't make too many individual eye-catching features in the small space of your garden— it will be too distracting and you will forever feel uncomfortable in it. Do not have niggling little features—think of the whole *always*.

Try to use some unifying items throughout. Let us suppose you have chosen to use an oblong-shaped slab of simulated stone: use it to edge your path, to edge the top of a wall, and then to edge the tread of some steps.

Later on we will look at various constructional details and we will discuss the flowers, shrubs and trees that I have used and suggested.

When you decide which plan most coincides with the shape, size and aspect of your own garden, please bear in mind this very important law: *All gardens must seem to grow naturally and seem to belong naturally to the site on which they are made.*

15

Chapter 2

Know your boundaries

Fences. Walls. Hedges.

Your garden, be it large or small, will have boundaries. If it were me I would find it difficult to decide if an old wall or an ancient yew hedge were the best boundary. Your actual boundary might even be an adjacent abattoir, but let us not despair! Fences you may have; old, old hedges, unkempt and decrepit. You may have chain-link fencing, as with a tennis court. Your choices are almost limitless.

Fences If your fencing is of wood it could take the following forms. It could be the old-fashioned overlap elm or oak fencing. This is easy to cover, gives good shelter, and is impervious to intruders. Larch lap panels are somewhat similar and cheaper, but not so lasting. A more modern note is struck by the American-looking ranch fencing, usually painted white and useful for climbing plants, especially roses. A most pleasing 'period' look can be given by lattice fencing in panels. The advantage of the last two kinds of wooden fencing is that whilst impervious to dogs and strangers they will allow light and air through, which is helpful to the growth of plants in the adjacent borders. Remember—solid fences throw heavy shade.

Chain-link fencing is familiar to all who have played tennis in a public park. It can be covered by vigorous climbers, like the climbing rose (Rosa filipes 'Kiftsgate') for example, or the Russian Vine (Polygonum baldschuanicum). Chain-link fencing is also simulated in a plastic variety, in green or brown, made by Netlon. This is somehow kinder and will accept climbers more readily—rabbits, however, have been known to eat it voraciously! There is the more ordinary wire netting

used for chicken runs—this can be effective if it is used as a 'stiffener' for Lonicera nitida, the small glossy leaved hedge from the honeysuckle family. Then there are strands of wire stretched between concrete posts, but they have the jolly look of the concentration camp about them!

Walls What is a more pleasing sight than an old brick wall— ancient with lichens and old climbing roses? What an asset to a garden; particularly if you have an archway through it with an old wrought-iron gate to frame a vista of more garden beyond. (Even an oriole peephole into the next door garden, so long as they are enthusiastic gardeners and not nudists!) You can build a fairly old-looking wall yourself with old bricks (now alas at a premium), and then painting it with a mixture of old cow manure and water to encourage moss to grow on it. This mixture is a good thing to use on all new concrete in a garden (unless you want it to look sparklingly new). In this way, concrete balustrading can look like old stone in a year or so.

Walls can be made of concrete blocks, or blocks of artificial stone. This artificial stone is manufactured from real stone ground down and remoulded and is very effective and aesthetic—not as good as using real stone—but very much easier to handle because of its more regular manufactured shape. Pierced blocks manufactured from concrete also make a decorative wall. They are the cement industry's answer to those gloriously beautiful, lace-like screens the Moors made in Spanish gardens of long ago. They are clumsy and mass-produced compared with their inspirational origins, but very pleasing, effective and easy for a handy amateur to erect. (Remember, though, that they make a fairly heavy wall when erected and need good foundations.)

Depending on what part of the country you live in, real stone walls are beautiful and, if indigenous, marry very well into a gardening scheme. I do implore you, dear Reader, not to import some foreign stone into your area. As an extreme example, let us not have shiny Aberdeen granite in Sussex— the stone you use, or the simulated stone you use, must be that of the area where the garden is to be made. Dry-stone walling, if it is to be of any height, really needs an expert to build it—this is where flat stones are used one upon the other, fitted in so cleverly that the 'stone hedge' will stay standing, through sheer weight and expertise, for a century. They are much easier to build as a retaining wall for a higher or lower level of earth and are not then beyond the patience of a dexterous amateur. And they will also provide a home for many a rock plant, the roots of which you build in with the stones as you go along.

Hedges And what about hedges? If you want a sense of period and formality there is nothing better than a yew hedge.

It needs clipping but once a year, and it is amenable to being carved into all sorts of shapes (remember its use in topiary). Yew (Taxus baccata) is not used a lot because it is expensive and slow-growing. Expensive it is, but once flourishing, it is there for ever, and in my experience is not all that slow. Properly planted in trenches of friable soil mixed with well-rotted cow manure, with old turves at the bottom of the trench, and given a little bone manure occasionally, my plants, about $2\frac{1}{2}$ feet high, grew in my Sussex garden to a 6-foot-tall hedge in six years. Put the shrubs in when the ground is warm in October—never let them get dry and sprinkle them frequently with water if you have a dry spring and summer, and they will flourish. I did not trim these bushes at all for the first three years, then I just shaped the sides with the shears and the tops were lopped with the secateurs. This was done in August so that all the cuts had healed over by the first autumn frosts. A yew hedge is a gloriously dark foil for brightly coloured flowers growing in front of it.

Beech hedges I'm fond of. They grow fairly quickly—they need trimming only once a year and they hold their russet leaves for the whole of the winter. Their soft green, slightly hairy, new young leaves are one of nature's spring miracles.

The Leyland cypress (Cupressocyparis leylandii) hedge is cheap and the quickest growing conifer of all. It has grey-green foliage—but there is also a golden variety now. Thuja plicata is the best conifer hedge for trimming.

Holly is evergreen and impervious even to your neighbour's bull. It is slow-growing—and beautiful.

Privet—oh do not have a privet hedge—you need to trim it at least three times a year and it takes so much goodness out of the soil. Have a golden privet bush as a single specimen somewhere, though, and you'll love it. Lonicera nitida, the Chinese honeysuckle I've already mentioned, has small glossy dark leaves and is a sort of superior privet-like hedge, but it needs lots of cutting.

Now, here are a few suggestions for shrubs to use as hedges but they will not like being shaped in the formal fashion of the ones I've already recommended. Berberis stenophylla has dark green leaves, spikey branches and pleasantly scented small yellow flowers. Prune it once a year. Escallonia mac-rantha has glossy evergreen leaves and red flowers in the summer; this hedge is wonderful for seaside gardens but is not hardy everywhere in the United Kingdom.

Then there is the Pyracantha crenulata, an evergreen with creamy white flowers and red-orange or yellow berries.

What about Rhododendron ponticum for a hedge? R. ponticum is the wild one with pale mauve flowers. It is very hardy, will need plenty of room; it does well in shade, but needs an acid soil.

Planning The Small Garden

Ranch fencing used as a boundary for the garden I designed for the Chelsea Flower Show in 1978

A Suffolk garden; walls and paving used with imagination in an enclosed space

A dry wall of Mucklow fabricated stone

A pierced concrete wall and patio

Then there could be rose hedges. The sweet briar rose grows quickly, can be trimmed if you like, and after rain it will perfume the air with the essence of an English summer. This is Shakespeare's Sweet Eglantine. Its Latin name is Rosa rubiginosa. The floribunda rose Queen Elizabeth is too tall for a rose bed, is lovely at the back of a mixed shrub border where it will grow to 15 feet high, but it makes a good flowering hedge. Give it a short run only as it is too startling for hedging a whole garden. Old shrub roses are particularly good for hedges.

If you need a high wall of foliage then a thin shrubbery of the right conifers, evergreen shrubs and small trees is most effective and will certainly blot out the local gas works! I have contrived a positive phalanx of greenery in my own garden.

When we are considering hedges there are the small low hedges which can be trimmed. Choose from box, cotton

lavender (Santolina), Old English lavender, some heathers and Berberis thunbergii 'Atropurpurea nana', which is the low-growing, purple-leaved berberis, and rosemary, though I'm not keen on trimming this (I like the odd sprig on my roast lamb too much to cut it back drastically!). The dwarf variety of mock orange (Philadelphus 'Manteau d'Hermine') planted 2 feet apart will make a gloriously-scented hedge up to 4 feet in height. I love this, and only trim it once a year by taking off the flowered shoots (it does lose its leaves in the winter though).

An effective little wooden fence to define a boundary

Hedges are not necessarily used for boundaries and may be used to cut up a garden into separate sections. They are invaluable as screens for a windy site—wind filters through a hedge and lessens its force, whereas a wall just deflects it. A hedge will reduce the wind's speed for a distance six times as long as its height. Thorn hedges are especially good for shelter against wind *and*—they are impervious to cattle!

23

Chapter 3

Setting the style

Near the house. Terrace. Patio. Paths. Levels. Lawns.

Facing page:
Part of the
garden I
designed for the
Chelsea Flower
Show in 1980
with a paved
patio or terrace,
which with its
greenhouse
forms an open
air 'bridge'
from the house
to the garden

One cannot go immediately from a house into a garden. There must be an intermediate atmosphere of neither house nor garden—a garden room—an open air extension of the house as it were. It is advisable to step from the house (in this glorious climate of ours!) onto a hard, easily-drained and quickly dryable area. Some garden designers call this a patio. I would rather call this area a terrace, although I admit this does envisage balustraded vistas of some stately home! If your small garden is particularly tiny it might be best to treat the whole area as an outside 'room' and pave it over, with trees, climbers, shrubs and plants as a decoration of its stony bones, so to speak!

If, however, your garden is large enough, then this terrace part will come between the house and the garden proper. It is a useful way to give your garden a different dimension—and according to your garden's shape it can be curved or straight; preferably it will be higher or lower than the rest of the garden and will be connected with it by some steps—again, to make an interesting feature. The different levels can be delineated by a low hedge, a wall, a retaining wall, or a balustrade: all according to the style and 'period' of the garden you are intending to fashion.

Now what are these hard, easily drained and quickly drying surfaces to be made of? I personally love old bricks and above all, I love old York paving stone—but this is the most costly. If you order old bricks from a gardening contractor or a builder then they will be expensive. So, sidle along with your most engaging smile to a demolition contractor who is

hastily knocking down a piece of Old England and you might get (subject to the cost of transport) your old bricks quite reasonably. York paving slabs are another matter and the building and gardening trades are now all well aware of their value. Try derelict railway stations—sometimes the platforms were made of this lovely material.

There are so many forms your terrace may take. You can 'cobble' the surface, which is the insertion of cobble stones in cement. You could crazy-pave it—this is the fitting, as in a jigsaw, of random broken pieces of paving or flat stones. You can use stone 'as natural', or squared-up. You can use simulated stone slabs which come in myriad sizes, shapes, textures and colours but please do not use anything too brightly coloured. Let the flowers and foliage give you your colours. (Remember also to choose a colour and texture to go with the walls of the house and surrounding countryside.) Even granite sets can be used effectively. Not only consider the actual materials you can use, but also the patterns that can be made. For example, if you are using bricks for a path, a herringbone pattern may be created. With so many diverse materials and so many possibilities of designs and patterns one's mind boggles as to what decisions to make. Guidelines here might be 'small areas demand small patterns, and large areas should be treated with a broader brush'. Remember that you can have curves to soften a geometrically square site, and vice versa, and remember too, that every so often one of the squares in your pattern can be left, or several of them can be left, for use as a flower bed and filled with earth. You can use grass and short hedges to alleviate and soften borders and shapes. Topiary, suggesting formality, is often used most effectively in this part of your garden which must be more formal than the rest because it is so near to the rigid lines of your house. The Cement Marketing Board have a whole range of imaginative ideas on paving and how to treat paved areas.

When constructing your terrace remember that it should slope slightly away from your house so that rain and storm water are not held between the terrace and the walls of the house. Similarly, when dealing with paving and soil borders next to the walls of a house, make sure that everything up to the soil line is lower than the airbricks and dampcourse of the house.

Here might be a good place to warn you also not to put trees which will grow eventually to large forest giants too near the foundations of the house. There is talk at the moment of building regulations to prevent the use of certain trees in suburban gardens. Common sense is the thing. Poplars grow quickly—so do Willows. Roses and various climbers like Wisteria, Honeysuckle, Virginia Creepers, Jasmine, Ivy are all right, but some small conifers eventually become large conifers and some grow to a great size quite quickly. Some of the indigenous Maples grow quickly for example. An acorn produced an Oak tree which I found quite difficult to move from the side of my house after only five years of growth.

Paths Whilst we are concentrating on hard surfaces we will discuss paths. In a small garden one might consider that paths are a wasteful use of valuable space and it would therefore be better to use stepping stones or grass paths or lawns to get you from place to place, but paths are extremely useful in splitting up a garden into several portions, and they are also invaluable in helping to camouflage awkward shapes.

If you are to make your garden look larger and more interesting than it is, then it is essential to split it up and to give it a 'what is round the next corner?' appeal. This can be given by the right-shaped paths, be they curved or straight. As you design, have in mind this desire to lead the visitor on. Imagine taking your first visitor on a tour round your garden. This way you will take him to some focal point and bring him back some other way so that he is suitably entertained by different terrain and different plants, views and vistas (no matter how small).

A useful example of how a path can help a garden is the trick of a straight path which is wider at the nearer end, and narrower at the distant end to give a false perspective and a greater illusion of distance. (This can be further enhanced by a formal planting of shrubs on either side. For example, Irish Yews, where the nearer ones are larger than the distant ones, which get progressively smaller.)

Levels Levels mean so much to a garden. Each part of your garden that is higher or lower than the other enhances the design because by splitting up the areas you create a more pleasing vista. As your levels change, so must your paths vary. Each set of steps (even if it is only one step) can be different shapes and sizes, thus adding to the character of the garden.

Sometimes there is an opportunity of placing a gate or an archway or an arbour at the points of change. In the same way that we can create different textures and types of paving for the terrace, so can we vary the shapes and sizes of the paths.

Make the paths to last. Make them so that they drain and do not contain puddles, and make them only where they are necessary to get from place to place, and where they are essential to give an added 'something' to your design.

Grass paths are delightful but they are a constant source of irritation if they are used too much and, in consequence, get bald or muddy. It's not a bad idea to 'reinforce' a grass path with stepping stones.

Planning The Small Garden

Lawns Lawns are an important part of any garden. The green expanse is restful to the eye and makes a wonderful backdrop (as we say in the theatre) to the shapes, textures and colours of your trees, shrubs and plants. Some gardens will be too tiny for a lawn—some garden owners do not want, or have not the time, energy, machinery or desire for the maintenance of a lawn; but where there is room I do advise one. Lawns are so helpful in giving shapes (beds and borders can be carved out of them so easily and so effectively) and the English climate is ideal for a beautiful lawn. Remember that with a small garden you will have the time to have a well-tended lawn to give the rest of the garden a sense of maturity and tranquility. If you would make your lawn the envy of your neighbours here are some helpful hints.

It is important to start well, to dig the site of your lawn thoroughly. Drain it if necessary, break up the subsoil and

give yourself an excellent topsoil. If the lawn is to be formal, then levelling is the next important step. This can be done with the aid of a spirit level and a number of wooden pegs. If a lot of levelling is to be done, beware that you do not remove the topsoil of one part and expose the subsoil. If extensive levelling is necessary, take the topsoil off, store it elsewhere in a heap, level the subsoil and then bring the topsoil back. Use a long straight piece of timber as your straight edge to put your pegs in about 10 feet apart. Then level with the aid of the straight edge and spirit level.

Turfing makes a good quick lawn, but seeding is ideal as various kinds of seed are sold for the differing uses of the lawn, from the finest 'Cumberland Turf', used for bowling greens, to the coarser seeds containing rye, for playing fields. Late summer, autumn and spring are the best times for sowing. You should allow the site to settle for a few weeks before

Outside my house I have created a terrace and a pool set in the lawn

Planning The Small Garden

In my garden: steps leading down from a lawn to make a feature of different levels. These steps are similar to those used in the fan-shaped garden (Plan 9, page 108)

sowing, as newly levelled ground needs to find its final level. Then check the levels and make good. Mark the lawn off into strips about a yard wide, as you are about to sow so many ounces of seed per square yard. This is usually marked on the packet as it varies with the kind of seed, but about 2 ounces per square yard is the average amount. You need to cotton the seed bed to scare birds. Choose a dry day but make sure the seed bed is of a very fine damp tilth. After sowing, use a finely-toothed rake to scratch the surface by about a half-an-inch. Scatter dry soil over the whole surface—dry molehills are ideal for this—then lightly roll. Make sure the surface is no longer damp or the seeds are likely to stick to the roller.

If the weather remains dry several days after sowing, you will have to water—but do it very gently with a very fine rose—don't pressurize all the seeds out of the ground. Remember—only a gentle sprinkle.

Weeds will appear after about three weeks and so will the grass. Hand weed, walking very gently over the grass, and this gentle pressure, so long as it is dry when you do it, will help the grass. When the grass is an inch high you can lightly roll it. When it is 2 inches high, roll again, and later in the day gently 'top' the grass with a very high set mower—$1\frac{1}{4}$ inches at least. It's got to be a sharp mower and it's got to be the right sort of day or you will, with a blunt mower on damp soil and grass, tear the new grass out of the ground. Mow regularly from then on—frequently with the box off so that the clippings will go back into the ground and help fertilize the new grass.

If you are going to turf a lawn, prepare your ground in the same way—lay the turves as you would the bricks in a wall—in other words, bond them so that the end of the second row of turves comes to the middle of the first turf in that row. This way you do not get one long straight join in any place across the lawn. Tread in each turf and use a plank to stand on. Work fine soil into the cracks. Remove the more blatant weeds as you lay each turf.

If you are to renovate an old lawn, hand weed and then use a lawn sand to remove the smaller weeds. Give a good top dressing of compost and fertilizer. If the lawn is waterlogged, insert drains. Also see to the level and, if necessary, take out whole turves with a turf cutter and insert sifted soil beneath. If you use a straight-edged plank for this the light showing underneath will denote the declivity. If the edges of an old lawn are ragged—a foot from the edge cut a length of turf along the whole edge. Then turn this turf around the other way so that the newly cut good edge is now the outside edge. Fill in the now ragged inside edge with sifted soil and beat the newly-laid turf well down. Sow seed on the bare patches and your new edge will be magnificent in a couple of weeks.

Chapter 4

Planting your garden

On being a miniaturist artist with Colours and Textures.

Facing page: In a corner of my rose garden, showing the Chicago Peace roses three years after planting

So you have decided firmly on the shape of your garden, on its divisions and on its format, style or mood. The divisions are made by paths, walls, hedges, that is, the structure of the garden. All of this has now to be enhanced and decorated with the plants suitable to the surroundings. It is with the plants that you will make your colour schemes and your variations of texture. As Gertrude Jekyll, the famous Victorian garden designer and authoress, has advised, we must now use 'a beneficence of overgrowth'. The amount of material we have to choose from is bewildering so we must use restraint. We must have colour—and colour not only through the whole spectrum but through a whole spectrum of seasons too. There must be contrasting foliage both in colour and texture; some of the foliage will be deciduous and will be gloriously different in spring and autumn; and some of the foliage will be ever-green and will give us interest even in the depths of winter.

We will deal in later chapters with trees, deciduous and evergreen; then shrubs in the same way; and then we will discuss plants of all kinds, be they perennial and permanent members of our household or just friends who drop in for a season like the short-lived but very colourful annuals and half-hardy annuals and biennials. In a small garden careful selection is of paramount importance. If we are to have a few of anything then it is only right and proper that we should have the very best available. Limited for space as we are, we may have to pay particular attention to the amount of shade, aspect, climate and soil. With a broad canvas we can afford to be a little slapdash with the way we throw the colours about,

32

but being, as it were, miniaturist painters, we must endeavour to be perfectionists. We must offer each plant the best possible conditions for its development.

The range of trees, shrubs and plants now available, as you can see on a walk round any large garden centre, is so enormous in variety that the beginner can easily be overwhelmed by this bewildering amount of choice and must be guided as to what is possible and practical for his own site. The folly is to try too many kinds and varieties as the result then is an unsatisfactory spotty effect. A more pleasing look will come from bold groups of happily situated robust plants. In devising clever colour schemes we must not forget the whole picture, and we must constantly strive for a unified and harmonious whole. With plants and trees readily available from all quarters of the globe, the prospect is staggering and bewildering. Try and make each of your pictures bold in scope, though not in scale. Be definite. Do not try too many distractions in a tiny space.

In a way, my Capital Radio Garden at the Chelsea Flower Show in 1978 (Plan 14) might be considered fidgety in that I have bothered perhaps too much with the colour schemes. But have I? Look at the plan on page 119 and follow me. On my right as we come down the steps from the terrace we have plants (A) of coppery red and blue colours, which gradually shade to (B) where we have a bold group of plants of white with white and yellow variegations and white and yellow flowers and foliage with silver foliage. Group (C) is a bold collection of mauve and blue, shading through dark red to brighter reds of group (D), to oranges and then yellow. Almost a spectrum of colour in a small space; several of the plants in groups of three, five and seven; the shrubs in so small a space being single specimens but their foliage and flowers marrying into the general colour scheme. At the same time there are enough evergreen and conifer shrubs here to create interest in winter, although on second thoughts (and who does not have second thoughts when gardening), I could have improved upon the winter scene.

The gardening notebook Talking of second thoughts, it will not come amiss here to talk to you of one of my fads and fancies. Do please have a gardening notebook. The volume does not need to be anything very special in itself, though it needs to be large enough and strong enough to be permanent. It could be anything from a hardbacked exercise book to a leatherbound volume with lettered sections. When your garden is flowering at its best, you say to yourself 'It would be so much better if I moved those reds nearer to those oranges —or that variegated holly would look so much brighter against a darker background'. Then you go on your way and by autumn the bright summer picture has receded in reality and also in your mind. You forget, and the following summer you are thinking the same thoughts and you realize that you have done nothing about them. Put your thoughts down month by month into your gardening notebook and then remedy the mistakes at the right time of the year when moving can be done. Also in your book you will note down all plantings of permanent plants and trees and the date. (To put down the prices of things is too dismaying in this inflationary age!) You ought to record where you got your plants from for repeat orders (or otherwise!). If you see an article in *Popular Gardening* or perhaps the daily or Sunday paper which appeals to you, cut it out and stick it in your book. Pieces from catalogues, the odd photograph or two, leaflets from the Chelsea Flower Show, varieties you intend to order in your annual seed list; there are a thousand uses for your gardening notebook and what a gloriously nostalgic volume it becomes through the years! Mine contains a list and plan of 400 plants for a herbaceous border I planted 40 years ago. (I have since moved four times during those 40 years and I still have plants in my present garden taken from that border.)

Plant with contrast in mind In a small garden the difference in the shapes of plants and their leaves and the way they grow is of more importance than in a larger garden. Plant with contrast in mind. A tall shrub next to a prostrate one or a spreading one. A shiny evergreen like Fatsia japonica next to the feathery silvery fern-like foliage of an Artemisia arborescens is an example of good contrast.

Use silvery plants and white plants in between colours you think might clash. Use silvery plants with pink and mauve; again, silver is equally effective with white and yellow. Use mauves and blues with plants of coppery foliage. Use variegated leaves of white and green and yellow with white flowers and cream and yellow flowers. Pale blue is especially good with white. Red and orange and yellow all go well together when you need to heat up the colour of your design. I would not use these last colours in a part of the garden I needed for rest; I would choose instead white and silver and mauve.

In the same way there are scents in a garden which go well together and some which 'clash'. Also you can wish that the flower of a pelargonium, so bright and effective, would add perfume to its charms—you can do this by giving it scented neighbours: for instance, plant Cherry pie—the deep-heliotrope-flowered one—in amongst the dark mauves of 'Lord Bute'. Plant mignonette amidst calendulas.

Scented plants—I mean plants with scented foliage like sweet briar, those scented foliaged pelargoniums in pots (there are some on the terrace near the burnt-out ruin at Nymans in Sussex)—are even more valuable in a small garden where we need to concentrate every effect.

Chapter 5

Trees for a sense of space

Evergreen and Deciduous. Conifers.

Facing page:
White flowering
cherry blossom
enhances the
smallest garden
and by leading
the eye to the
sky gives an
illusion of space

The only limit for trees in a small garden is that of size: no forest giants, please! Plantings of small trees in a small garden because they are to scale give the whole picture a sense of space. Trees lead your sightline upwards and towards the sky—thus helping to give the illusion of space. Pencil-shaped trees (fastigiate) are useful—perhaps in groups to lead the eye upwards, or at the end of a border as an exclamation mark. They give height to a flat site. Horizontal, spready trees help sometimes to marry or disguise different levels.

If you plant a group of trees the tendency will be to plant too closely. I still do this after 40 years as a gardener. When you plant you must have in your mind's eye what it will look like in 10 or 15 years' time; what part of your garden it will transform by shade and shelter, and will this permanent blob of colour be exactly what you want? Will its own particular form or habit achieve what you want it to do: hide a neighbouring eyesore perhaps? In a small garden a tree or clump of trees, especially if evergreen, can be the focal point from which you will design the rest of the garden. Also let me remind you again that if you are re-designing an old garden do *not* precipitately cut down trees or large shrubs—you may be able to use them. Prowl round your plot, beetle-browed, pondering on this permutation and that, until you come to a properly considered final solution with, I hope, as little carnage as possible.

If your house is new and modern in style you can choose from a plethora of plants. If your house is old you must choose plants in period; for example, for a distinctly Victorian

36

Planning The Small Garden

Villa, a monkey puzzle; if it is Tudor or Jacobean or William and Mary, yew hedges would be in keeping; while a Georgian House *demands* a cedar of Lebanon. You must always try to establish a mood. I feel it would be wrong, for example, to have apple trees, as in a small orchard, with plantings of evergreen conifers. The apples suggest a farm-cum-smallholding or roses-round-the-door atmosphere, and the conifers suggest a different villa, or suburban type, or even a forest atmosphere. You could use both in different parts of the garden, but they must be in smaller gardens of their own in which you will then have two separate moods or atmospheres —not a bad idea, incidentally, on a narrow long site to cut it into two in this way.

Here are some trees admirably suited to the small garden:
Deciduous trees Whitebeam (Sorbus aria). This has lovely silvery leaves in spring.

Mountain Ash (Sorbus aucuparia). Feathery leaves and white blossom, followed by red or yellow berries.

Standard Apple Trees. Choose your favourite variety for eating but make sure it is either self-fertile or is accompanied by a 'mate' which flowers at the same time. Rosa filipes 'Kiftsgate' is a very quick growing and vigorous rose to grow in and about a mature apple tree.

Hawthorn. Both red and white. The red one takes several years before it flowers.

Japanese Cherries. There are so many it is impossible to know which ones to mention. There are small trees of all shapes, ranging from low and spreading to tall and erect. The flowers are single, semi-double or double, and vary in colour from dark pink through cream, creamy yellow to purest white. They are easy as to soil and there is an added bonus in their rich autumn leaf colouring. Pruning is rarely necessary, but if you need to do so late summer is the best time so that the wounds can heal before winter.

Prunus japonica Amanogawa (Serrulata erecta). The poplar-shaped tree, very suitable for small gardens. Pale pink flowers in late April/May and the young leaves are greenish bronze. P.j. Tai Haku. Known as the great white cherry, the flowers are single and pure white. P.j. Kanzan. Medium-sized tree with ascending branches which spread with age. The flowers are large, showy and purplish pink. The young leaves are coppery red. Miss Sackville-West thought this tree vulgar, but it's very popular and possibly you can enjoy the one next door and then use the extra space for some other variety! P.j. Ukon. A robust tree of spreading habit. The flowers are semi-double, pale yellow tinged with green. These are especially effective against the young bronze foliage. P.j. Yedo Zakura. A small upright tree, flowers are carmine when in bud and almond-pink when fully open. P.j. Pink Shell. Small and elegant, with spreading drooping branches and shell pink flowers. For a white spreading tree choose Jo-nici. It is single and scented.

For a weeping cherry choose Prunus subhirtella pendula. It is a slender weeping tree, with inconspicuous pink flowers.

For an early flowering tree of moderate size the Almond (Prunus dulcis) is a good choice; the flowers are pink and single in March and April. Alba has white flowers and Praecox flowers in February.

Prunus cerasifera Pissardii is the purple-leaved plum. It has dark red young foliage turning to deep purple.

Prunus avium Flore Plena is the double white wild cherry.

The flowering Crab Apple (Malus) is almost as beautiful as the cherry and flowers a little later, thus prolonging the flowering period, and, of course, its shapes are different, making a contrast with the cherries; most valuable of all, there are the decorative fruits later in the season.

Malus Lady Northcliffe is small, with carmine-budded flowers opening to pink then white, and the fruits are small and yellow. Malus purpurea has dark purplish foliage and rosy crimson flowers grown in profusion, while the fruit is a light crimson purple.

The Siberian Crab is Malus × robusta—either Red Siberian or Yellow Siberian according to the fruits; the flowers are white or pinkish. If you would like a weeping crab apple try Malus sieboldii with pink flowers and red or yellowish fruit.

Malus hupehensis has white scented flowers in May and June and yellow fruits.

Whilst we are considering fruit, I personally am in love with the Mulberry (Morus nigra). It is a small slow-growing tree, and gives a great sense of period to your garden if your house is old; the leaves are heart-shaped and downy beneath, and the fruit—most edible—are like large black-red loganberries.

I know I have advised you against forest trees in a small garden. If, however, your garden is small but not overcrowded by surrounding buildings, then a small group of Silver Birch trees is most agreeable. One with conspicuous silver bark and showy catkins is Betula caerulea-grandis Blanch. Betula pendula Youngii is a good weeping variety.

The next two recommendations are small trees with fern-like foliage which maintains its glorious yellow/green spring-like colour for the whole summer. They are wonderful for brightening a dark corner or to be seen against dark foliage, such as a Yew, dark green conifers or copper beech. One is the False Acacia, Robinia pseudoacacia Frisia, with bright yellow leaves; and even more exotic is the Gleditsia triacanthos Sunburst. Both these trees, as well as always looking freshly spring-like, flourish well in the polluted air of towns,

Left: Ornamental cherry—a good specimen tree for a small garden

Right: Rosa filipes Kiftsgate growing through an old apple tree

and they are not at all particular as to soil. If I were allowed only one tree in my garden it would be either one of them.

If you want a 'pleached alleye' of trees, then the red-twigged Lime, Tilia × europaea, is the one which is amenable to trimming and shaping. A row of these, suitably trained (pleached), will hide all sorts of unsightly neighbourhoods.

A gloriously light-hearted look is given by the yellow and white and green leaves of Acer negundo—the variegated Maple, and it is lovely if surrounded by variegated and white blooming plants and bushes. And quite different, heavy, dark red or purple, like a well fed cardinal full of port, is Acer pseudoplatanus Atropurpureum. If you grow through it and over it a Clematis—Clematis languinosa 'Blue Gem' which has large sky-blue flowers from June to October—your neighbours would be green with envy. Do you want a tree whose leaves in the spring are pink and yellow and whitish green? Acer pseudoplatanus Brilliantissimum will give this to you and so will A.p. Leopoldii, only this one remains splashed with pink for the whole season. I shall include the gloriously coloured Japanese Maples when I discuss the shrubs, although some of these do become small trees. I've left out Laburnum because the seeds are poisonous and might be fatal to small voracious children.

You will remember I have advised against a weeping willow in a small garden. If, however, you do yearn avidly for one

40

and still want to preserve the foundations of your house, have a weeping pear (Pyrus Salicifolia Pendula). Its leaves are willow-shaped and silver grey and its blossom purest white *and* it is slow-growing! Another tree for a small garden is Amelanchier (poetically the Snowy Mespilus) which has white blossom in spring and glorious red foliage in the autumn, a tall, small, graceful tree.

Those, then, are some suggestions for the small deciduous trees for your garden. I can only recommend a few here—but visit some of the famous gardens with your gardening note-book in spring, summer and autumn and perhaps decide for yourself but do remember that some flourish only on acid soil and some on alkaline.

Evergreen trees Now we must look at the evergreen trees. The trees which will furnish your garden in the winter as well, and for this reason are possibly the most important. Yew is the native evergreen which immediately springs to mind. It can be very large but it grows slowly. There is the Irish fastigiate Yew which eventually gets to tree size. Holly (Ilex aquifolium) similarly becomes a tree and there are variegated kinds, Silver Queen, and Golden King. These last two are excellent for brightening a dark corner. There is a weeping holly too if you need a sad Christmas (Ilex aquifolium pendula). Bay makes a tree, either formally the mop-headed kind you put in a tub, or slow-growing pyramid type that is

Woodland garden at Knightshayes, Tiverton, showing a Cedrus deodar grown almost as a weeping tree

the laurus nobilis, the Laurel of the ancients. There is also one with golden yellow leaves Laurus nobilis Aurea. (It would give a creamy look to a rice pudding!) Eucalyptus are evergreen but not hardy everywhere.

There are many evergreen conifers, which have a great variety of colour and form, and they can provide a valuable and fascinating addition to any garden, especially in the winter. The conifers can roughly be grouped as follows:

Abies—the silver firs.

Cedrus—the Cedars.

Chamaecyparis and Cupressus—cupressus is less hardy.

Cryptomeria—an attractive medium sized feathery tree which changes colour in the winter.

Juniperus—hardy shrubs or small trees, some prostrate, some horizontal and the largest about 26 feet high.

Picea or Spruces—(a Christmas tree is a spruce) some can be enormous forest trees.

Pinus—the pine trees, usually large trees, but there are some smaller ones suitable for our use.

Taxus—the Yew.

Thuja—Thuja placata make magnificent hedges when trimmed and need a well drained situation.

Abies concolor can grow to 160 feet high—it is a dense fir tree and a specimen in a corner makes a good dark green screen, and it is well furnished at the base.

Cedrus atlantica 'Glauca'—it does grow to well over 100 feet high but it is slow-growing and if used as a specimen tree in a small garden is very beautiful with its wonderful blue spring foliage. Of course if and when it does get too large in 20 years' time you will have to find it another owner but its great beauty is worth the heartbreak. Slower growing is the 'Aurea'—a golden variety. The Cedrus deodara is a graceful tree with drooping branches—there is a golden and slower growing variety, C.d. Aurea.

Chamaecyparis is a small genus with many popular species, admirably suited to the small garden. The golden ones are very useful to lighten a darkish corner, although most golden plants, unless in a well lighted position, lose their brightness and tend to become light green. C. lawsoniana 'Lanei' needs a south-facing position and is then good for summer and winter colour. C.l. 'Lutea' is less bright than 'Lanei' but has more feathery upright foliage. C.l. 'Stewartii' has wider spaced feathery foliage which is a golden green. The best of the blues for a small garden are: C.l. 'Columnaris' grows as a narrow pillar of bluish grey. C.l. 'Pembury Blue' has silver-blue foliage. C. pisifera 'Boulevard' has well known feathery silvery blue foliage. It does not grow very large—maximum 12 feet—and is slow-growing. It makes a good exclamation mark at the end of a border. C.l. 'Fletcheri' is a good green cultivar with dense soft foliage up to 22 feet high. C.l. 'Erecta Viridis' is a good green and so is C.l. 'Ellwoodii'. Once you know the potential size it is perhaps best to visit a garden centre and choose which kind of shape and foliage appeals to you personally. If you choose anything from a garden centre you have a wonderful opportunity to make sure that your purchase is of good quality and, most important with a conifer—symmetrical.

Cryptomeria japonica 'Elegans' is browny green in summer and its delicate feathery foliage turns to copper bronze in the winter. I would not be without my tree.

Cupressus Macrocarpa is the well known Monterey Cypress. It is subject to damage in severe weather though the golden variety 'Goldcrest' is hardy. This excellent quick-growing plant has been much superseded by Cupressocyparis leylandii, which is very quick in growth, trims well as a hedge, and is perfectly hardy. It does root somewhat shallowly for its height and is sometimes wrenched from the ground by a gale. Its top is sometimes broken off if it is planted on a draughty site, but such is its resilience and speed of growth, it quickly recovers its shape if helped with judicious pruning. There is a golden variety which is slightly more expensive.

Of the Junipers only Juniperus communis 'Hibernica' really grows to tree size with attractive greyish foliage and Juniperus scopulorum 'Skyrocket', the narrowest and most pencil-like, grows to 22 feet with grey foliage and is a quick grower.

The picea genus or the spruces do not look happily at home in a small garden as trees, although there are smaller, pros-trate shrubs which are very useful. There is a very blue tree which looks sufficiently artificial to look at home in the necessary formality of the smaller garden as opposed to a mountainside, and that is the Colorado spruce, Picea pungens. It grows to 30 feet high.

The Pines are all too large or too small, except perhaps for Pinus sylvestris 'Beuvronensis' which is particularly golden in the winter when you need it. (It grows to only 9 feet high.)

Taxus baccata 'Fastigiata' is the Irish Yew which is dark green and grows to 16 feet or so, and T.b. 'Fastigiata Aureo-marginata' is the golden form of Irish Yew which needs to be in a sunny position for its full glory.

Thuja occidentalis 'Lutea Nana' is slow-growing up to 14 feet of golden yellow feathery foliage and is erect in habit. T.o. 'Lutcescens' will grow to 15 feet and is slow-growing, colour is a white light yellow-green in summer and creamy in winter, and is shaded darker as the leaves reach the centre of the tree. Thuja plicata is the one used for hedges, is dark green and will grow to 200 feet high! You have been warned!

Chapter 6

Shrubs for all seasons

Evergreen and Deciduous. Shrubs. Climbers. Roses.

We will now discuss a few shrubs for the small garden, remembering as we do so that a shrub, unlike a herbaceous plant, does not need dividing or staking or renewing. For this reason be careful over the positioning of shrubs—vigorous growers not to overwhelm slow-growers, the sun-lovers and the shade-lovers properly sited and the shrubs you choose right for your kind of soil—acid or otherwise.

As a general rule you will find evergreens are slower growers than deciduous shrubs, and for this reason when you are planting you can either plant the deciduous shrubs a proper distance from the evergreens, allowing for their full expansion, or you can buy cheap fillers-in, like brooms, tree lupins, and so on, which can be dispensed with later and which will probably be in decline in a few years anyway. It's not a bad idea to put a group of quick growers next to each other at the right distances and slow growers in another group so that no individual shrub is overwhelmed. In a small garden it's best to choose plants not only for their bloom and their scent but also for their decorative foliage; if you have all three and fruit as well you have chosen a star performer indeed!

When planting your borders aim at informality. A tall tree here, there a short one, a deciduous pair, and then a conifer. The conifers and evergreens will give the whole silhouette of your planting an interesting shape so vary your heights, vary the textures of your plants and, of course, vary the colours.

A small garden is often successful using small conifers and heathers exclusively. The combination of shapes, colours and forms of small conifers, together with the brightly coloured

foliage and flowers of heathers (heathers have such a long period for flowering if you use groups of different kinds). These gardens are also very labour-saving as a lot of the material used is ground cover and will suppress weeds. The expert in this kind of gardening is Mr Adrian Bloom at Bressingham Gardens, and he has kindly let me have some pictures of this sort of garden, including a view of his own.

All year round greenery Some evergreen shrubs for the back of a shrubbery are Camellias (acid soil). Camellia japonica is evergreen and hardy. The colours range from bright red to white—there are singles, semi-doubles, Anemone form and doubles. It is best to plant them in a woodland site as diffused overhead shade is ideal or, alternatively, plant them in the shelter of northern or western walls so that the early morning sun does not follow the frost, which browns the flowers. The clone C. × Williamsii Donation has an attractive branching habit and semi-double large pink flowers, and is my favourite. They are good for tubs and pots and positions of importance on a terrace. Ceanothus are often evergreen and there are various kinds to grow from April to late September. Most popular is A. T. Johnson, flowering both in spring and again in the autumn. The Cotoneasters are easily cultivated and there are many kinds. Cotoneaster glaucophyllus vestitus gets to 13 feet in height, flowers in July and the fruits colour in late December. C. franchetii has semi-evergreen sage-like foliage, graceful in habit and has orange/red berries.

Elaeagnus pungens Maculata is a shaft of sunlight even on the darkest winter's day. Every evergreen leaf has a bold golden splash in the centre, which is butter-yellow and shines in the sun. It reaches 15 feet high. Sometimes the bush tries to revert and produces ordinary green shoots. Cut them back at once. Escallonias are shiny evergreen plants (which flourish especially at the seaside) with prolific flowers in colour from white to dark red. No scent, but very useful for hedging.

Euonymus japonicus 'Ovatus Aureus' is another happy sunny yellow bush which needs little care but full sunshine to make sure of the brightness of the variegations.

Garrya elliptica has foliage of a very deep green and in the winter and spring, long jade-green catkins; they are useful dark background foil for a brightly flowering plant.

Hebes are evergreen and a little tender. H. armstrongii is the bright variegated one for the back of a sheltered border. (It does well under the protection of a weeping tree.)

Ilex aquifolium (common holly), we have mentioned as trees. I.a. Pyramidalis Fructulutea is a holly with yellow berries.

Kalmia is an evergreen which grows to 6 feet. It needs very

acid soil and has pink-icing coloured flowers—it also needs semi-shade.

Golden privet Ligustrum vulgare 'Aureum' is a beautiful plant to grow as a specimen in the border. Magnolia grandiflora can be a large tree but it is slow-growing and needs the shelter of a wall. It has large laurel-like glossy leaves and gloriously lemon-scented flowers from July to September. You must have one no matter how small your garden. Plant it near the house on your terrace and savour its succulent summer scent! I'm not sure whether to include Mahonia in the taller shrubs or the medium ones, but you should certainly include it in your garden. It has rich green holly-like foliage which turns to russet and bronze in the winter. It grows usefully in semi-shade. Mahonia × media 'Charity' has flowers which, in fragrance and appearance, are similar to the Lily-of-the-Valley, from December to February. M. bealei is more upright with smaller flowers.

Olearia macrodonta, growing eventually to 10 feet high, comes from New Zealand and has white daisy-like flowers in June and rich green leaves, which are white felted on the underside. The whole plant is faintly scented. There is a later flowering one, O. × haastii, for July and August.

Osmanthus grows eventually to 6 feet and has dark green small leaves to set off to perfection the small white flowers which are scented like jasmine and look somewhat similar.

Pieris will grow to 15 feet in time (see Sheffield Park and Nymans) and to 6 feet in as many years. It is evergreen and has scarlet bracts in the spring but also flowers with a Lily-of-the-Valley type bloom and scent. Pieris formosa forrestii 'Wakehurst' is a brilliant red and there is a much smaller, slower growing one, Pieris japonica Variegata with cream and green leaves. This shrub is only for acid soils.

Pyracanthas will grow in any soil. Orange Glow is vigorous and dense and P. crenatoserrata 'Knap Hill Lemon' is a strong grower with lemon yellow fruits.

There are some very good tall rhododendrons for those with acid soil. A pH 5 soil is about the best for rhododendrons This selection will grow quickly.

White—Geo. Hardy. Sappho.
Yellow—Butterfly. China. Harvest Moon.
Red—Fred Waterer. Grand Arab.
Scarlet—J. G. Millais. Lamplighter. Garibaldi.
Crimson—Cynthia and Lady Longman.
Pink—Corry Koster. Midsummer. Pierre Moser.
Deep Pink—Betty Wormald. Lady Eleanor Cathcart.
Mauve—Arthur Bedford. Lady Decies.

'Pink Pearl' is a very popular one but not quite so quick in growth. In a small garden you must be sure of the right place and it might be better to have a slower growing clone—all of

Planning The Small Garden

Left:
Cistus
purpurens with
its shocking
pink flowers

Right:
Pieris Flame of
the Forest is
doubly valuable
with scented
white flowers
and later on
bright red
bracts

the above have reached 8 feet or so in ten years in my garden.

Viburnum tinus is evergreen and eventually reaches a height of 10 feet or so, but is too slow-growing to put a small plant at the back of a border. It's very generous with its pink and white flowers all the winter through. I would not be without mine. Also evergreen is V. rhytidophyllum with creamy white flowers in May with red fruits which turn to black later. V.p. roseum has pink flowers.

I omitted to mention the large-leaved laurel (Acuba japonica) as it is really too large for our sort of garden but the very yellow one might be useful.

Some smaller evergreen shrubs for the front and middle of the border must include the evergreen Azaleas. These are generally known as the Japanese Azaleas and include Kurume, Kaempferi and the Vuyk hybrids. They are slow-growing, very generous in bloom (some very small blooms and some quite large—even with bell-shaped flowers) in April and May. I will not confuse you with named varieties. The best thing is to see them in flower in containers at garden centres, make your selection, and buy on the spot.

Berberis is a widely differing group of plants and among

Skimmia
japonica is
long flowering
and has a
pleasant scent
with berries to
follow

Left:
Golden privet—
cheap and
common little
hedge plant it
may be but as a
specimen in a
border in my
garden it is
unrivalled

Right:
Elaeagnus
pungens
maculata
is a shaft of
sunlight even
on the darkest
winter day

the evergreens are B. darwinii with small holly-like leaves and yellow flowers. B. × stenophylla is used a lot in hedges but as a specimen plant it grows gracefully amongst other shrubs in long arching sprays with lots of yellow flowers in April and May.

Box, or buxus sempervirens is the edging plant used in knot gardens as a low hedge. B.s. Aureovariegata has leaves striped and mottled with creamy yellow. B.s. suffruticosa is the dwarf form best used for edging.

The Heathers are dwarf evergreen shrubs, which can give a long period of flowering as there are so many varieties and species. Many of them have brightly coloured foliage.

Mexican orange blossom (Choisya ternata) has dark shiny leaves on a rounded shrub with sweetly-scented flowers through spring and summer. It does best in full sun. Cotoneaster conspicuus Decorus is a small plant admirable for the front of a border or rock garden. It is generous with its berries and 'Highlight' is of medium size, has white flowers in May and large orange red fruits. C. hybridus Pendulus has evergreen glossy leaves which are borne on long prostrate branches with brilliant red fruits in autumn and winter. This

Rosa filipes
Kiftsgate in my
garden, with its
fragrant
clusters of
small white
flowers

49

can come in the form of a small weeping tree. C. 'Pink Champagne' (Watereri Group) is a large vigorous shrub with pink fruit. C. 'Salmon Spray' is medium sized with salmon red fruit.

Daphne is a genus of fragrant shrubs (usually deciduous) always needing good drainage. Daphne acutiloba is evergreen, long leathery leaves with white sweetly scented flowers in July. It also has large bright scarlet fruits. Daphne laureola is the spurge laurel, a native of this country and flowers with fragrant yellow blooms in February and March.

Euonymus fortunei 'Coloratus' is a trailing evergreen which is good for ground cover in sun or shade and turns purple in the winter. E.f. Kewensis is suitable for the rock garden.

The Cistus is a rock rose and largely a Mediterranean family, so you will need to take cuttings each year for fear of losing some. For the same reason have them on a sunny, well-drained sheltered part of the shrubbery. I love them, not only for the flower but for the fragrance of the plant itself, especially C. ladaniferus which grows to 5 feet, has large crinkly white flowers, sometimes with blotches of maroon at the base as you look inside the flower. C. × cyprius has a blood-red patch. C. albidus has leaves covered with feltish down—pale lilac-pink flowers which are single-rose-like. C. × purpureus has what I call 'shocking pink' flowers. C. 'Silver Pink' is a very hardy hybrid produced by Messrs. Hilliers. These shrubs have an atmosphere of old gardens about them, difficult for me to describe. They settle in well and grow quickly (and die quickly, too, I'm afraid). They help a garden to look mature and to 'smell' old and established.

Two small hebes are H. Carl Teschner with dark green leaves and purple flowers and H. pinguifolia Pagei with silver-grey leaves and white flowers.

Hypericum coris is a dwarf evergreen useful for rock gardens or dry walls and has golden yellow flowers during the summer.

Lonicera nitida 'Baggessen's Gold' is a small evergreen used for hedging but in this gold variety you could use as a specimen plant.

Lupinus arboreus is the Yellow Tree Lupin. It is evergreen and short-lived—a good filler-in. Golden Spire speaks for itself and so does Snow Queen. It is easily grown from seed.

Dwarf evergreen Rhododendrons are excellent for the small shrubbery—remember that they are surface rooters and will need a mulch of peat and leaf mould every year. They are also most particular about having a neutral to acid soil. It's good to give a mulch in the autumn to keep the surface roots from frost damage. ICI pulverized and composted bark is an excellent mulch. R. williamsianum is approximately 3 feet high and has glossy brown foliage and shell pink flowers in April. With soft green hairy leaves mucronatum has white (Bulstrode) or mauve flowers (Ripense) and is 3 feet. Another white is R. leucaspis. Lava Flow is a good hybrid, 2 feet high with scarlet bell-shaped flowers in summer. R. Ovatum has rosy red flowers in summer and makes a 4-foot round hummock. R. prostratum is 1 foot and the colour of rich magenta. R. scintillans forms a $1\frac{1}{2}$ foot hummock with tiny leaves and violet blue starry flowers. I'm very fond of a Kurume Azalea called 'Palestrina'—it is a splendid low-growing, small shrub with large white flowers.

Senecio greyii is a silver-leaved plant from New Zealand which spreads its branches and luxuriates in sun. It has yellow daisy-like flowers but it is for the silver foliage that you have the plant.

Skimmia japonica is a neat dwarf shrub with fragrant flowers (S.j. Fragrans) while the best one for berries is S.j. Foremanii.

Santolina—the cotton lavender, is a short, silver feathery plant. S. chamaecyparissus is good and there is also S. neopolitana which is whiter and more feathery. It has tiny yellow button flowers but I cut mine off at once as they only die off rather nastily and cutting back the plant helps to keep it in trim and the younger foliage more silvery.

There are several deciduous berberis, the best being B. Thunbergii Atropurpurea with mahogany-coloured foliage.

Azalea mollis is the deciduous one in a range of colours. There are also Ghent Hybrids and Knap Hill Hybrids. They range in colour from white and pale cream to yellow, orange, flame and pink. Azalea ponticum is the deciduous species and is very pleasantly fragrant and has bright crimson autumn leaves. They prefer light shade. Azalea oblongifolium grows to 5 feet high and is deliciously fragrant of clover blossom—in colour a silvery pink and white, tipped with a darker pink.

Deciduous shrubs The Japanese maples or acers are first because they come so alphabetically, but they are first, too, because of their beauty, even though they do not flower. They must have an acid soil and they prefer shelter. As the buds unfold, the leaves are very tender green and there is a soft downiness about them like a beech bud unfolding. A. palmatum 'Atropurpureum' is deep crimson. Its tender ruby foliage, with the spring sun through it, is most beautiful and, then in the autumn comes magnificence again. Acer palmatum has bright yellow-green foliage to start with and A. dissectum 'Atropurpureum' has finely-cut purple leaves.

Azalea occidentale is deciduous, fragrant, flowering pale pink, pale orange and yellow, with funnel-shaped flowers in June. Don't ever mix deciduous Azaleas with Rhododendrons.

I know they are the same family but their colours and forms are so different they never look happy together.

The Buddleias are very valuable shrubs for producing a quick effect, and indeed some of them will double their height in a year. They can become over-large if used too generously —but they can be propagated so easily, and they seed themselves so easily too, that there is no great drama in yanking one out when you have got tired of it.

Buddleia globosa is almost evergreen (it is in the south and west) and hardy everywhere. It grows to a large bush: up to 15 feet—it develops in a denser way than the other Buddleias in that it grows up more than splaying out. In May and June it is covered with orange flowers rather like small oranges or woollen balls which smell richly of honey.

B. davidii, from west China, is the popular one; in southern gardens its flowering time begins in June, up north, perhaps July, but it always depends so much on the position and the soil—and the loving care! But a Buddleia does not need too much fussing; it's a robust creature. The flowers are fragrant and range from white through pinks and reds to purples—all strong, dramatic colours. B.d. 'Alba' is white; B.d. 'Black Knight' has long tapering flowers of deepest violet; B.d. 'Charming' is lavender pink; B.d. 'Border Beauty' is more crimson than purple. A sub-species (or different variety might be more correct), B.d. nanhoensis, has narrower leaves; a more delicate look altogether has B.d.n. 'Pink Pearl'; and B.d.n. 'Royal Red' is red-purple. Buddleias are much loved by butterflies and even in the days of sprays and insecticides they bring a galaxy of colourful guests to your garden.

Caryopteris Heavenly Blue is a small, showy, late-summer flowering plant with aromatic felt-like leaves and blue flowers which are especially valuable in the autumn. Grow it in well-drained soil and full sun.

Ceratostigma griffithii has blue plumbago-like flowers in late summer and autumn.

The Cydonia or Chaenomeles speciosa is the ornamental quince. Best on a wall, it also makes a good small shrub on its own. It has orange and red flowers with yellow stamens. There is a white one called C. speciosa 'Snow'. You can make quince jelly of the fruit. It's supposed to be the forbidden fruit of the Garden of Eden, in which case Adam had magnificent molars!

Chimonanthus fragrans or praecox has rather insignificant brown and yellow waxy flowers with a marvellously strong scent during the winter months. It needs the support of a wall.

Cneorum—you will not believe this somewhat tender plant with bright, silvery, silky leaves about a foot high at most— excellent for rockeries. It has pale pink or white convolvulus flowers and needs full sun and good drainage.

The Cornus family are the dogwoods. Some are grown for

their scarlet or bright yellow stems and should be pruned hard every other year in March. Cornus alba has rich red stems; C. amomum purple stems; C. stolonifera flaveramea has yellow stems. C. mas has yellow flowers in February. Cornus alba Elegantissima lovely variegated leaves in the summer and C. alba Apaethii has leaves of bright lime-green.

Cotinus coggygria 'Royal Purple' has rich purple leaves and is a very useful and showy plant. Its flowers from a distance give the idea of wisps of smoke and it is known as the Smoke Tree.

Cotoneaster horizontalis is invaluable for north and east walls with its fan-shaped, herringbone branches, dark red foliage and red berries later on.

Crataegus are the May or Quickthorn trees.

Cytisus are the brooms—easily grown from seed and not very long-lived, but quick-growing and good fillers-in-ers. All have arching branches and small sweet pea-like flowers. In April C. × praecox is creamy white; C. × kewensis is wider spreading as a good ground cover; C. scoparius named clones are all colours from pink through red and salmon to almost purple. A near relative is Genista pilosa. Genista lydia is dwarf broom with arching stems of golden flowers which may spread up to 6 feet—with me it has spread less than a foot in five years. Genista hispanica is the Spanish gorse and it's about 4 inches high at most, forming dense prickly mounds covered with masses of flowers in May and June. Genista aetnensis 'Mount Etna Broom' is 4 to 5 feet tall with large yellow flowers in July.

Deutzias need room. They are floriferous deciduous shrubs. D. × magnifica is 6 feet high with white flowers. D. × rosea is an attractive pink. Forsythias are surely known to every gardener. Yellow flowers smother the bare branches from March and April. You prune after flowering.

Daphne mezereum is the well-known scented shrub, flowering in February and March with deep purple flowers.

Eucryphia—white flowers with bold yellow stamens from July to September. Grows best in light shade.

Fuchsia. I shall mention only ones which have been grown successfully out of doors. Some are often cut to ground level by the winter, but they will come again vigorously the next spring. We are all aware of the splendid hedges of fuchsia in Devon and Cornwall, Ireland and Western Scotland, but for less fortunate folk they are so easy to propagate from cuttings that, given a cold frame, you need never be without a whole lot of your favourites ready as understudies (in my profession) or replacements. They don't mind either sun or shade but they do need a well-drained soil. I very much like, and find quite hardy, F. magellanica 'Versicolor', which is a small spreading shrub with leaves of a greyish-green which start off by being red. The flowers are scarlet and violet—2 feet high at the most with me, but may possibly grow taller. It is also found in other areas where the winter does not bring it to the ground. F. procumbens is a trailer, and F. 'Display' has large flowers of carmine and rose-pink.

Lavenders come from the Mediterranean countries. L. lanata is the whitest and woolliest of them all; it flowers from July to September and comes from Spain. L. spica is the ordinary common or garden lavender. It has many varieties: L.s. 'Alba' with white flowers—I have got it in my white garden but it seems to grow more slowly than the others. L.s. 'Hidcote' is a compact plant with a very floriferous habit and dark lavender spikes; L.s. 'Nana Alba' is white and minute and could be used on the rockery. There is also a pink one, L.s. 'Loddon Pink' and from Gertrude Jekyll's garden we have L.s. 'Munstead', blue lavender, and L.s. Nana 'Munstead Dwarf', excellent for a low edging round a bed.

Hamamelis is the Witch Hazel which brightens our gardens in December and January with its ragged yellow blossoms, so bravely defying the weather. H. × intermedia 'All Gold' is excellent. There is also 'Orange Beauty' and 'Ruby Glow'. The most popular is the Chinese Witch Hazel H. mollis 'Gold Crest'. Also the best yellow is H.m. 'Pallida'.

Hydrangeas come roughly in four kinds. There is the Hydrangea hortensia which is the large mop-head variety, and the Lacecaps which produce a flattened centre to the bloom, round which there is a border of ray florets. H. anomala and H. petiolaris are the climbing hydrangeas which cover vast areas holding on to trees or walls like ivy with aerial roots. The flowers are of the lacecap variety and somewhat insignificant. The plant seems to stand still the first two years and then suddenly it is up and away 10 feet or more in a season. They love north walls, so are very valuable. The fourth kind is H. paniculata—quite a large shrub with large creamy-white flowers a little like lilac but on the ends of the branches, like buddleia. You treat it rather like buddleia by cutting it back in a similar way. With hydrangeas it is important to remember that you should cut back and thin out the old shoots immediately after flowering; it is from this year's new shoots that you will get next year's flowers and if you cut these back you will not get any next year!

Hypericum—the shrubby St John's Wort—is a valuable contribution to the midsummer scene. It is most floriferous with large buttercup yellow flowers. H. calycinum 'Rose of Sharon' is an excellent ground-cover plant and can be used in full sun or shade—to my mind, although it is the most despised and commonest of the St John's Worts its flower is the largest and most beautiful. Trim it lightly in the spring. H. elatum 'Elstead'—has several small flowers at the end of each stem. H. Calycinum is attractive in that its flower almost entirely consists of the anthers and the petals are small.

Helichrysum serotinum is also known as the Curry plant—it has silvery leaves and is highly aromatic. H. petiolatum is a silvery trailing plant, wonderful for tubs, but is not hardy.

Kerria japonica is about 6 feet high, needs the support of a wall and has flowers like a double buttercup.

Kolkwitzia amabalis likes any soil and is a blaze of pink and cream flowers in May and June.

Magnolia × Soulangiana has large white tulip-shaped flowers suffused with pink and purple. M. × s. Lennei are flushed strongly with purple. Magnolia Stellata is early with small strap-shaped petals and is a good small garden shrub.

Tree paeonies: Paeonia delavayi and p. suffruticosa—the Moutan Paeony with many clones ranging in colours from white, yellow, pink, red and mauve are beautiful plants with lovely foliage which is susceptible to night frost in spring.

Blue flowers and silver foliage are most beautifully displayed by Perovskia atriplicifolia and are excellent in the front of the mixed border.

Philadelphus is the mock orange, often called, wrongly, syringa (this is the name for lilac) and is one of the easiest and most gloriously scented of the summer deciduous shrubs. All soils are suitable and they come in many sizes. P. microphyllus is a beautifully scented feathery dwarf shrub. P. Belle Etoile grows to 9 feet with a flushing of purple at the base of the flowers. P. 'Virginal' has an almost bell-shaped flower. But if you want a plant which stands out in the border because of its glorious sulphurous yellow-green foliage choose P. coronarius Aureus.

Potentillas are some of the most generous shrubs I know. There are tall ones and short, spreading ones. The tall kinds P. fruticosa have white or yellow flowers. A new red has been introduced, P.f. Red Ace—I think dark orange would be a more faithful description. The shorter spreading ones for the front of the border—very good ground cover—are P. arbuscula with deep yellow flowers; P. fruticosa mandshurica is a dwarf low-spreading with white flowers.

One of the disadvantages of lilac as a shrub in a small garden is that the bush is so drab and nondescript when it is not flowering and so glorious when you are gathering it down an English lane. Syringa vulgaris is a large vigorous shrub and the following are a few representative cultivars. Single lilac flowers—'Madam Francisque Morel'. Single white flowers—'Mont Blanc.' Single red—'Pasteur.' Double lilac—'Michel Buchner.' Double white—'Madame Lemoine' and double red—'Mrs Edward Harding'.

The viburnums are a large and talented family. Viburnum opulus 'Sterile' is the guelder rose or snowball tree; V.

carlessii one of the most popular medium-sized shrubs, with downy leaves and strongly scented flowers. V.c. 'Aurora' is pink and very fragrant. V. grandiflorum produces pink flowers in February and March which are very fragrant on a medium-sized bush.

Weigela produces foxglove-like tubular flowers in May and June, W. 'Bristol Ruby' being a rich red while W. florida variegata has pink flowers and white and green leaves. This is a most beautiful plant all the summer for its foliage alone.

Beautiful climbers There are many climbing shrubs suitable for small gardens. Clematis come readily to mind—the species being easier to grow than the large-flowered hybrids. Clematis montana is excellent for north walls and growing through trees. Flowers are smallish, white and star-like. C.m. rubens is pink with bronze foliage in spring. Some popular hybrid large-flowered Clematis include C. 'Nellie Moser', a pale mauve-pink with crimson bar and flowers May to September. C. 'Jackmanii Superba'—violet-purple July to September. C. 'Ville de Lyon' is deep crimson and flowers from July to October. And for a spectacular double violet-blue flower C. 'Vyvyan Pennell' which also produces single flowers in the autumn. Clematis are best planted where their heads are in the sun and their roots in the shade. If you want it to grow up a tree, plant it well away from the tree's roots.

The quick growing rhododendrons, which I planted two feet high ten years ago

A large flat stone over the roots gives a cool root run in a small garden where shade might be difficult. They are gross feeders and there is a fatal and puzzling disease called Clematis Wilt. One morning your plant may be flourishing in the sunshine. An hour later it may appear dead. When this happens cut it immediately to the ground—the stricken creature may then grow from the root—but alas, not always. A species Clematis tangutica is easily grown and has yellow lantern-like flowers in July and later in the season.

There are many worthwhile Ivies (Hedera): Hedera helix 'Buttercup' is the best yellow common ivy. H. colchica 'Dentata Variegata' is yellow, white and green and so is H. canariensis 'Variegata'—almost as if the leaves have been painted with water colour.

There are many useful Honeysuckles (Lonicera) too; Lonicera japonica is evergreen and rampant and deliciously scented, while for a brighter coloured plant choose L.j. 'Aureoreticulata'. L. periclymenum is our native honeysuckle and L.p. 'Belgica' is the Early Dutch Honeysuckle with larger redder flowers and to my mind not so fragrant.

There are the redly coloured vines: Parthenocissus, green in summer and red in autumn—and a very pretty variegated one is P. henryana. Polygonum baldschuanicum is known as the Russian Vine and I hesitate to recommend it in this book

Do not despise so ordinary a rambling rose as the American Pillar. Here it is growing with great charm in my garden

as it is so very vigorous. However, you may have some very ugly building which needs covering quickly—it is very attractive when in flower with a feathery creamy bloom—but remember to stand back quickly once it is established or it will have you! There is nothing to stop you have a fruiting vine in the open—'twill be quenching your thirst in a few years!

The Passion Flower will grow in a sheltered garden, and if you prune away damaged growth it will more than likely start off again in the spring.

Roses I have studiously avoided roses so far because they are such an important part of a small garden. I felt they should be treated on their own.

Consider a moment the Hybrid Tea and Floribunda roses. They are incredibly cheap and even with inflation as it is, have risen very little in price. They will last in good, full flowering order for ten years—longer in some cases. They do not need staking. In the case of some floribundas they flower for four months continuously—even the HTs repeat themselves these days at least three times in a season. They need manure. They need pruning. They are very sturdy items in a garden 'plagued' with dogs or children. They come in every colour except blue. Their diseases are few. Tell me of another shrub or plant that has all these admirable attributes. Add to these the fact that there are fanatical rose breeders all over the world improving roses all the time and giving added fascination to your hobby by producing new varieties every year, and you realize how richly rewarding rose-growing can be.

We may not have room for a rose garden on its own—although if we are to have a 'separate garden' in order to improve a long awkward shape then a rose garden is a good excuse for a separate enclosure. Then you will use the Hybrid Teas and the Floribundas. If you have room for separate beds, or part of your whole design contains separate beds, then Hybrid Teas or Floribundas should be your choice to fill them, given the right soil and sunny position. If, however, you can only use roses in amongst your other trees, shrubs and flowers, you will find the Hybrid Tea rose a bit formal—it does not marry-in well. The occasional Floribunda will—there is nothing that looks better in a mixed border than a group of three white Floribunda roses 'Iceberg'; or a few tall 'Queen Elizabeth' roses at the back of a shrub border towering to 12 feet or so. But the best roses to use in a mixed shrub border are the old-fashioned shrub roses. Their colour, the colour of their foliage and their growing 'habit' can all be used to advantage in a mixed border.

Shrub roses come in all sizes from 2 feet tall to 12 feet and some are so unusual in appearance they can become a focal point in a garden. Their chief disadvantage is many of them only flower once, but some are repeat flowering and most of them have decorative foliage and hips in the autumn. Their colourings are mostly pinks, mauves, creams and whites, dark purple and maroon. The yellow rose was only brought in as recently as 1900. No pruning is required other than to keep them within bounds and to cut out very old or dead wood.

The true species roses have single flowers. Rosa gallica is the one from which most of our garden roses are descended. It is thought that the Rosa gallica was crossed with a musk rose and the result was R. damascena—the Damask Rose. A Damask Rose crossed with our native Dog Rose then produced the Alba Rose. The Centifolia roses are the result of many other crosses; these are those lovely blousy old roses you see in the Dutch still-life flower paintings—these eventually sported the Moss Roses. From China came Rosa chinensis, which was a perpetually flowering species and it is the crossing of this with our other roses which has given us the Bourbon roses and from these came the Hybrid Perpetuals. Then Tea roses were imported from China, crossed with Hybrid Perpetuals and thus we arrive Q.E.D. to the modern Hybrid Tea rose of today. The Rugosa roses are a separate species imported from China and Japan. And now to confuse you further there are many 'new' old-fashioned shrub roses which our modern breeders have presented us with, like 'Nevada' and 'Constance Spry', which have all the beauty of the old with some modern advantages of vigour and colour.

The above paragraph is a brief history and a précis of shrub roses culled by me from *Shrub Roses for Every Garden* by Michael Gibson and published by Collins. For those of you who are keen to know more about the old-fashioned roses this book is a must.

Today we must recognize, especially in the context of the small garden, the Miniature Roses—these will be used where much shorter varieties are required and will flourish as bushy plants up to 18 inches in height with a profusion of miniature flowers. 'Royal Salute' to celebrate Her Majesty's Silver Jubilee is a good example—it is a fine rose-pink with fragrant miniature flowers.

Repeat flowering climbers, some of which are of recent origin, and some old favourites, fulfil many purposes in the small garden—they will clothe walls, screens, pergolas, pillars and trellises. The old Hybrid Tea climbing roses are still popular, particularly where a greater height is needed. And the ramblers are still in demand where a quick response is required, providing in a short time, and, alas, for a short flowering period, a mass of bloom and colour for arches, pergolas, summer houses etc.

Chapter 7

Flowers for a beautifully-blooming garden

Annuals. Half-hardy Annuals. Biennials. Perennials
Heathers. Bulbs. Dahlias.

If you are creating a new garden then expense is of prime importance, and so is the desire for immediate results. Sometimes your requirement is for a temporary effect—a mass of flowers in a part of the garden which in time will become, as your plan evolves, something else, and in the meantime you dislike seeing it as a bare space. Your remedy in this predicament is to sow annuals and half-hardy annuals. Annuals are grown by sowing out-of-doors from March till June in the place where the plants are to flower. Some can be sown in the autumn to flower in the following early summer, but all annual plants die after flowering. Half-hardy annuals include most of the summer bedding groups; they are usually sown under glass, raised under glass, and then planted out in the open garden when there is no longer a danger of frost. Some can be sown out-of-doors later in the season but they will have a short growing life as the first autumn frost will cut them down. Biennials are sown one year to flower the next and are then discarded, although some, such as Sweet Williams and the biennial verbascums, can be used for several seasons.

The general cultural procedure, if you have the time, is to dig the ground over well in the autumn so that the frost can get at the soil and break it down, and then to sow in the spring where plants are to bloom. No manure is required so long as the soil is in good heart, as annuals often prefer to flourish on a poor soil. Compost always helps a poor soil in texture and

substance, and remember you will need a fine tilth for sowing. After hoeing and raking the soil to provide this fine tilth, you can sow the seed broadcast over the area you need your plants to grow, or in drills. It is essential to sow the seeds thinly and never deeply—the ground should only just cover them. Indeed, with some of the very fine seeds there is no need to cover at all. When the seedlings are an inch or so high thin them out a few inches apart, choosing to leave the strongest and more vigorous seedlings. Then subsequent thinning out should eventually leave your remaining plants spaced out at about three-quarters of their final height (e.g. a plant that is going to finish up to 1 foot in height should be 9 inches apart from its fellows). It always seems to me a great pity to throw the seedlings away; so long as you do your thinning out in showery weather when the seedlings are small, you can transplant these thinnings to some other part of the garden. If your garden is on a windy site you must place twigs at intervals amongst the plants. These supports will be hidden when the plants are fully grown—hazel twigs (short lengths of pea sticks) and brushwood are the ideal material.

Annuals All the following are easy annuals to grow, can be bought in packets with cultural directions, height etc. to say nothing of the most alluring picture of the annual in question on the packet.

Alyssum. White or violet, fragrant, mat-like plants. Good as fill-ins on the rockery.

Anchusa Carpensis. Like a large Forget-me-not.

Calendula. The pot marigold, an old-fashioned flower with many new hybrids and refinements.

Coreopsis. Annual daisy in yellow shades.

Candytuft. Seeds can be bought in self colours or mixtures —several sowings a season provide constant colour.

Chrysanthemum. The annual is vigorous with bright banded tricolour flowers.

Clarkia elegans. Tall graceful sprays of double pastel-shaded flowers of white, pink and mauve.

Convolvulus Major. Morning Glory, blue-flowered climber.

Cobea Scandens. Treat as half hardy annual—mauve or white bells. A great climber.

Cornflower. 3 feet down to dwarf varieties, blue, pink and white.

Cosmos. A tall fern-like annual either pink or white daisy-like flowers. There is now a yellow five-petalled variety.

Eschscholzia. The Californian Poppy—used to be orange, yellow or white. Now there are Harlequin Hybrids from Carters, all colours except blue. Also from Dobies, 'Ballerina' which has double-fluted variegated flowers.

Godetias. Have been vastly improved too in the last few years—the dwarf bedding godetia being useful for edgings and to fill in empty spots in the rock garden. The godetia needs sun. There are tall varieties which are useful for cutting. If I owned a hotel and needed flowers in a small pot for each table in the dining room, I would grow a succession of godetias the whole summer through.

Gypsophila. Is a plant I would grow for the same purpose. It is a complementary flower—like a feathery fern might be—to other flowers in an arrangement, and in the border it makes a most interesting mound of dainty, pure white or pink flowers. You sow it the previous September to give you early flowers, and then from March to June to give a succession throughout the season.

Larkspurs. Are a kind of annual Delphinium. Sow in September. Whites, blues and pinks.

Lavatera. The annual Mallow. Good to grow amongst Lupins which will be over in July and then go on till late summer.

Linaria. The annual toadflax, a sort of yellow snapdragon.

Linum. The Scarlet flax.

Love-lies-bleeding (Amaranthus candatus) is a plant much used by flower arrangers. It is very good for the tops of walls so that its long dangling tassels can drape themselves over the edge. They have an odd Victorian look about them. The crimson one has slightly reddish leaves too, particularly when young; the green one has light green tassels: sometimes these drooping furry tassels are longer than the plant is high, if I make myself crystal clear? And this is why I plant them near the edge of a wall so that they may hang over.

Mignonette. Greenish flowers with a red tinge and very fragrant.

Nasturtium. Is a climber or a dwarf bushy plant. Flowers are sometimes double and fragrant. Ranges in colour from mahogany through brightest reds and oranges to palest yellow. The poorer the soil the happier the result.

Nigella. Love-in-a-mist. Blue flower in a mist of green feathery foliage. Alas you can now get pink, white and a dirty dark mauve, but I'll stick to blue.

Poppies. Annual Poppies are Shirley, and the biennial ones are Iceland Poppies. All lovely pastel shades from white through orange and yellow and red.

Sunflowers. The annual Sunflower is a magnificent giant redolent of old cottage gardens and very useful if you have an aviary as the seed heads are enormous. The various varieties range from 4 feet to 7–8 feet in height. I grow them against a wall with hollyhocks. When they are in need of water they look down on you in a scornful way, and when you have watered them they raise their heads to the sun and grow and grow and grow. No wonder Van Gogh could not stop painting them.

A beautiful
herbaceous
border in
Dublin
Botanical
Gardens—
impossible to
emulate in a
small garden
but it shows
how to mass
plants for
effect.
See Plan 6

Planning The Small Garden

Half-hardy annuals Half-hardy annuals are best sown in pots or boxes in a warm greenhouse or frame during February and March. The seedlings are then pricked out into other pots or boxes and are still kept in the warmth till April. In April and May they are gradually hardened off, but you cannot put them out into the open garden until all danger of frost is passed. One sees so many half-hardy annuals offered in boxes by shops in April whilst there is still a possibility of frost and you should, to my mind, not buy them until you can plant them out. Any interruption in their growth will spoil them and their chances of being 100 per cent successful as flowering plants. This goes for letting them get too dry as well.

Ageratum. Fluffy blue heads, lavender or Cambridge blue, if you remove dead flowers will keep flowering June/October. There is a new variety called 'Blue Surf' from Suttons which is lovely.

Antirrhinums. Are perennial but best treated as half-hardy annuals. They grow slowly and you must get your seed into boxes in February. There are many new varieties but the older, taller, fuller kinds are coming back into fashion. They are often subject to a rust disease and you should make sure if your area is subject to rust and then to buy only a rust-resistant strain.

China Aster. Is invaluable to keep your flower show going well into late summer. It needs to be sown in March. Here again, as with the Antirrhinums, there are many hybrid varieties ranging from dwarf ones to Hercules, doubles, singles ostrich plumed, and every colour of white, pink and blue—and in the Aster 'Unicorn' variety there is a yellow.

Begonia. Fibrous rooted begonia is treated as a half-hardy annual.

Cleome pungens. Grows to 3 feet high and has large pink spider-like flowers. 'Rose Queen' is the variety. A very well worthwhile plant.

Delphiniums. Can be treated as a half-hardy annual. You can then get your flowers in the summer when blues are at a premium—these are the Chinensis varieties and not to be confused with the rocket larkspur.

Coltness Dahlias. Are treated as a half-hardy annual, and by the end of the summer you will have tubers for use the following season.

Annual Pinks. Make a very good fill-in for bare patches in the rock garden—especially Dianthus 'Persian Carpet'. They are excellent for patches in paving and for edging. From Suttons a F_1 Hybrid called 'Snowfire'. You sow January to March in a heated greenhouse and plant out in late May for a June onwards display of large single white flowers with bright scarlet centres. Similarly, you can grow as a half-hardy annual (although it is a perennial) a new flowering deep crimson double carnation from Suttons called 'Crimson Knight'. The plants are dwarf, compact and beautifully perfumed. Plant out May or June for flowering in the autumn.

Helichrysum. Are everlasting flowers which, when cut and dried (hang upside down), will make excellent flower arrangements for the winter.

Heliotrope. Is the cherry pie with deliciously scented flowers. I plant mine round the base of eucalyptus trees and in hot summer the scent is wonderful. You can plant H. arborescens 'Giganteum', which grows 2 feet high with the silvery pink flowers of the newish short hollyhock (treated also as a half-hardy annual).

Lobelia. Is a carpeting plant used by the Victorians for bedding out—but in drifts of 2 or 3 feet wide is spectacular.

The Marigolds. The double African Marigold, the French Marigold and the tinier, dainter Tagetes are all much the same family, and all have had considerable attention from the seedsmen. You can get many shades of colour in the orange, mahogany, yellow range and they range in height from 2 feet to 9 inches. You sow the seed in heat in March and prick out, when big enough, into other boxes. You then plant out when the frosts are over into their permanent positions, when they will flower from July onwards. From Suttons there is a new Double French Marigold with bright red blooms (10 inches high) which become golden bronze as they mature called 'Queen Sophia', which is a good example of the new varieties which seedsmen are constantly evolving for our fresh delight.

Mesembryanthemum. Are only for dry and sunny positions, opening their star-like daisy flowers in sun with rich reds, pinks and purples. It is a carpeting or trailing plant. Be careful as you transplant because the stems between the succulent heavy leaves and the roots are thread-like.

Nemesia. Is a quick growing small plant up to 1 foot high in many colours used en masse or for edging.

Nicotiana. Is the tobacco plant. It is much improved these days, in that it will flower during the day as well as at dusk: but it is in the evenings that one notices the heavy fragrance. There is a lime-green flowering variety now that is in great demand by flower arrangers. If you are on a windy site tobacco plants are prone to falling over, so use the new dwarf varieties.

Penstemons. Are magnificent plants, and sown in a heated frame or greenhouse from January to March will give a wonderful display from July to late summer; then bring them in to the shelter of your frame for the winter.

Petunias. Are lovely plants for a fine summer but look sadly

**Left:
Contrast in
foliage—in the
foreground
hosta undulata
medio variegata
and hosta
sieboldiana at
the back**

bedraggled after rain. There are new spectacular F_1 Hybrids. I use a salmon-pink one with Cineraria Maritima (silver grey) very effectively. Suttons have a new spectacular variety called 'Grandiflora Blue Frost'. It is violet-blue with a pure white edge to the wavy petals of large flowers.

The Annual Phlox. Phlox drummondii has brightly coloured clusters of flowers and is an excellent bedding-out plant. It is easy and continuously flowering. These need a few twigs between them here and there to make sure they stand up.

The Gloriosa Daisies. Are a late summer delight and the giant tetraploid hybrids are special favourites of mine, with large single flowers 6 inches across, with conical centres and stiff stems. The colours are yellow and dark brown and chestnut and mahogany red, and petals are the texture of fine velvet

Salvia 'Blaze of Fire'. Is a good stand-by for creating a patch of brilliant red from June/October.

Salvia patens is intense gentian blue.

Salpiglossis. Is a much improved flower, as we have seen at recent Chelsea Flower Shows. They are now 2 feet high

with richly veined flowers, all colours from blue, yellow brown and pink, and looking as exotic as an orchid.

Statice. Is a half-hardy annual from the sea-shore. There are many pastel shades and they are not only attractive in the garden but as a dried flower they are a flower arranger's delight.

Night-scented Stocks as we used to call them, some coming in miserable single-bloomed spires and some very beautiful double flowered spires, all have a much prized perfume, particularly on a still damp day in mid-summer. Now you sow in gentle heat and the seedlings are a light or a dark green; the dark ones are singles, so you ruthlessly remove these and the light green-leaved seedlings grow up to be the desired exotic double-flowered blooms. You get them in packets of mixed colours or you can get packets of a definite shade, so that in bedding schemes you can be very selective and artistic. The lavender ones go well with a blue border, and the white ones are very valuable to fill in bare patches of a white garden. Seed can also be sown in a frame in June for winter sweet flowers in the greenhouse.

Centre:
Annual
nemesia, used
effectively in
a front garden

Right:
A pink
decorative
dahlia, so easy
to grow and
good in borders
in groups

Verbena. Is an attractive flower shaped a little like a small Sweet William. Excellent for filling in a bare patch in the front of a border.

Zinnias. Are a rather stiff-stalked formal-looking daisy in attractive colours from South Africa. It is best to sow in tiny peat pots in heated greenhouse as these plants do not like being transplanted. They come in all colours except variations of blue and mauve.

Biennials Biennials include Bellis (the double daisy used in spring bedding schemes); Border Carnations and Dianthus; Canterbury Bells; Cheiranthus (the Siberian Wallflower); Foxgloves (with the recent 'Excelsior' strains where the gloves are spaced all round the stem so the plant faces all ways at once); Honesty (with the silver seeds for flower arrangements and the mauve flowers in spring); Meconopsis baileyi is often listed as a hardy perennial, but like all true biennials once it has flowered it will give up the ghost, and an out of this world poppy ghost it is! Myosotis (which is the posh word for Forget-me-nots) is the loveliest of spring foils for Darwin tulips.

I treat Pansies as biennials, sowing them in the summer and cruelly throwing them away when they become straggly with exhaustion, after they have so generously bloomed themselves to death for me. Treat Violas in the same way as pansies. Viola cornuta 'Alba' is a much loved plant of gardening expert Christopher Lloyd, who uses it a great deal at Great Dixter. He says it particularly likes the heavy soil of our locality, and has a six months' long season. It also has a very pleasant habit of growing into and through other plants.

Penstemons we have talked about. The double Brompton Stock should be sown mid-summer for the next year's blooming, but you must winter your plants in a frost-proof frame. Sweet William is a biennial but it will live on for many seasons without becoming too tattered. The Verbascum bombyciferum is a biennial, and the first year if planted or sown in its permanent quarters will supply you with grey-frosted leaves of great size and interest before it flowers next year.

Wallflowers you sow in May and June; you then thin out and plant the seedlings out separately in rows in the kitchen garden 6 inches apart, pricking out the centre of the plants to make them bushy. Then when the dahlias have succumbed to frost you transplant the wallflowers to their final quarters to flower the next spring, and to delight you with their unforgettable spring-like fragrance.

Perennials These are the herbaceous plants which will stay with you year after year—they may need dividing—some of them every few years or so. If they do, you dig them up and choose the outside stronger parts of the old plant and discard the matted, exhausted centres. Most of them can be grown from seed but it does take a whole season—sometimes more—to get a fully established plant. To avoid a great deal of work it is perhaps best to only go in for perennials which do not need staking . . . but when your garden is a small one then you will often be looking for something to do. It is best to put stakes into, and around the plants, when they are still short in the spring so that they will grow up, through and round them. I hate to see a plant tied round (with string!) looking like a buxom farm female tied tightly at the waist. Hide all stakes. Yes, even with delphiniums and dahlias.

The range of perennial plants is vast. The cult of island beds of perennials (as opposed to the long herbaceous border) as advocated by Alan Bloom of Bressingham Gardens—together with the many new clones he has introduced—and the advice of Christopher Lloyd of Great Dixter especially in his book *The Well Tempered Garden*—have brought perennials into renewed favour. I can but recommend a few in so small a book as this, however.

Acanthus Spinosus, or mollis. Large architectural plants 3 feet in height with most decorative leaves and white and lilac hooded flowers.

Achillea filipendulina Gold Plate is 4–5 feet—with wide, golden, long-lasting, flat flowers and leaves fern-like and beautiful. A. Moonshine has silvery foliage and yellow flowers and is 2 feet. A. millefolium Cerise Queen is pink and low-growing, forming a useful mat for the fronts of borders and path edgings.

Alchemilla mollis has a nondescript yellow flower. It does not mind being dry under trees. Its foliage is attractive and it makes a good ground cover.

Aconitum (Monkshood). Long-flowering (the juice of the plant is poisonous so if you want poisoned arrows here's the very thing!). Either white or blue, 3 feet high, sometimes more—July to September.

Agapanthus (Lily of the Nile) is hardier than we are led to suppose. Flowers in blue or white tall lily-like flowers and strap leaves.

Anaphalis—grey foliage plant and the small white tufted little flowers grouped together like the head of a Sweet William can be dried for flower arrangements.

The Alliums are onions—so do not step on the foliage! A. acuminatum has rose purple flowers in June and is 1 foot high. A. giganteum is 4 feet high from May to June.

Alstroemeria (Ligtu Hybrids) The Peruvian Lily. Once established (it takes about a year in a sandy well-drained soil) it is a great sight with colours ranging from white through yellow to red and lilac and rose purple from June to September. Roots need to be 12 inches deep.

Planning The Small Garden

The beautiful effect of lilies in a border at Sissinghurst Gardens in Kent

Cottage near
Barnstaple,
Devon. A good
example of a
labour-saving
front garden
using annuals

Armeria is the Thrift. As I'm thrifty I plant Chives instead —the flowers are similar and you save space in the kitchen garden!

Artemisia (Lambrook Silver) is a tall (3 feet) silvery plant useful to break up clashing colours.

Aruncus sylvester—a noble plant needing an important position and lots of room—it can be 6 feet high and likes damp.

Anchusa 3 feet high with Forget-me-not-like flowers in June and July.

Japanese Anemone. Flowers either white or rose-pink and is like a wild rose—18 inches high. Flowers August onwards.

Aquilegia is the Columbine with some lovely new varieties.

Asters. Are the Michaelmas Daisies (amellus, and novi-belgii and novae-angliae) tall ones and dwarf ones, colours white and blue and mauve and red, from late August onwards.

Aster frikarti. Flowers from early July till end of season.

Astilbe—elegant plumes and finely laciniated foliage. They like damp. Bressingham Beauty has rich pink plumes 3 feet high. Fire is salmon-red, Irrlicht is white. There are also lilac and purple shades.

Astrantia has curious fine petalled flowers at mid-summer, strongly scented, and can be 6 feet high.

Bergenias. Good ground cover with reddish large leaves like elephant ears. Good company for Hellebores (Christmas Roses) about a foot high with pink or white flowers on fleshy stems in early spring.

Campanulas (Bell Flowers). Indispensable in any flower border, also ideal for the wild garden or amongst shrubs, where partial shade is provided. C. glomerata superba ($2\frac{1}{2}$ feet), clusters of bright violet flowers on erect stems. C. Lactiflora alba (3–4 feet), dense sprays of a multitude of white flowers, very elegant. C. Lactiflora pouffe (9 inches) makes a spreading mound covered with lavender-blue flowers. C. Lactiflora Prichard's Variety ($2\frac{1}{2}$ feet) has large heads of deep blue flowers. C. Lactifolia gloaming is pale lilac-blue, June, July—4 feet.

Catananche. Grey-green foliage and cornflower like flowers $2\frac{1}{2}$ feet.

Centaureas—large yellow, thistle-cum-cornflower like heads (related to Knapweed) 5 feet high some of them (C. macro-cephalia). C. montana is smaller with silvery leaves.

Chrysanthemum maximum is the Shasta Daisy large and white. 'Wirral Supreme' is double.

Coreopsis. Golden yellow starry flowers.

Crocosmia masonorum. With red flowers is a superior sort of Montbretia.

Dicentra spectabilis. The bleeding heart plant with feathery leaves 2 feet high May to June. Likes shade.

Dianthus. One immediately thinks of the white pink Mrs Sinkins with her double flowers bursting from their calyx. The seedsmen Allwoods specialise in many different kinds and you really should study their catalogue. There are also Border Pinks and Carnations in many different shades of pink and red.

Echinacea is the rudbeckia—daisy-like flowers from rose to purple with dark blackish cone centre 3 feet high.

Echinops—Globe Thistle flowering from June onwards. E. humilis Taplow Blue is dark blue and grows to 5 feet. E. ritro is 3 feet.

Eryngium is easily confused with the Globe Thistle—it is in fact the sea holly, which is ideal dried for winter decorations. E. tripartitum has metallic blue flowers and silver-grey foliage, and is 3 feet. 'Blue Dwarf' is smaller, 'Spring Hills', 3 feet, has deep blue thistles, 'Jewel' is violet and E. planum (4 feet) has masses of small blue flowers in branching sprays. E. variefolium has pretty marbled foliage near the ground, and erect branches of blue flowers at $2\frac{1}{2}$ feet.

Erigeron. The flowers—nearly all summer long—resemble Michaelmas Daisies. New varieties: 'Rotes Meer' (18 inches) is almost red and 'Schwarzes Meer' (24 inches) is lavender violet. E. Prosperity is a good double-blue.

Euphorbia. The Spurge. E. polychroma (epithymoides) has sulphur yellow heads in early spring 18 inches high. E. griffithii 'Fireglow' is red—3 feet in May.

Gaillardia. Daisy-like flowers of orange, rust and yellow. June to August.

Geranium. These are not to be confused with the Pelargoniums, which are the greenhouse flowers used as bedding-out plants. These are hardy and very different. G. endressii A. T. Johnson is silvery pink, 1 foot high and flowers continuously June to October. Johnson's Blue is 18 inches high and Russell Prichard is a magenta pink 12 inches and spreads, creeps and indeed climbs.

Gypsophila. Lace-like plant covered in white flowers. G. paniculata 'Bristol Fairy' is 3 feet and double white. This plant likes plenty of manure and a chalky soil.

Helenium—is like a coppery or yellow Michaelmas Daisy. July to October, 3 feet high.

Heliopsis. Golden Plume—double golden daisy-like flowers $3\frac{1}{2}$ feet high. Very showy.

Helianthus. H. 'Loddon Gold' is 5 feet with double flowers 4 inches across August to October.

Helleborus niger (Christmas Rose). White flowers tinged with green or pink—December to March. You cover with a cloche in inclement weather.

Hemerocallis is the day lily, very easy to grow to height of

Hypericum
Hidcote—a
valuable
contribution to
the mid-
summer scene

Examples of
contrasting
foliage in my
garden
Left:
Azalea, globe
artichoke and
golden yew
backed with
cupressus
Lawsonia
hedge
Right:
Variegated
apple mint in
front of a
monster
angelica

A tiny cottage
garden at
Selworthy,
Exmoor

77

about 3 feet—they flower amongst a large clump of strap-like leaves and range in colour from yellow to H. Morocco Red. H. Pink Damask is deep pink.

Heuchera. A little bit like a gloriously improved London Pride. 2 feet high, deep crimson flowers ranging in colour to pale pink. Look at the Bressingham Hybrids.

Hollyhock. 6 feet high of nostalgia for the cottage-type garden. Pink, dark purple and white. Also double ones.

Hosta. Wonderful foliage plants which grow in damp and shady positions. H. fortunei aurea marginata—large green leaves edged yellow. H. fortunei picta—leaves a mixture of green and yellow—turning yellow when mauve flowers arrive. H. undulata medio variegata—wavy leaves of green and white. H. sieboldiana elegans—blue crinkled leaves like enormous plantain leaves, hence Plantain Lily, its old name.

Iris germanica—the large showy flowered Iris in every garden.

Iris pallida aurea variegata—golden yellow variegated leaves.

Iris siberica—loves damp, excellent for edges of ponds.

Lavendula—See shrubs.

Lily-of-the-Valley. You buy them as root crowns after they have flowered and you'll never be without them, they spread and you love them for it.

Lupin—I would rather you treat them as biennials—they flower May to July and if you dead-head later in the season too. Colour ranges of all kinds. 3 feet.

Ligularia—tall yellow daisy-like flowers. L. Stenocephala is the Rocket and has spires of small yellow flowers on long black stalks in late summer.

Lamium. These are the variegated nettles and are very useful for growing in dry shade. There are pink, white and yellow flowers, all are low growing plants of variegated foliage.

Liatris spicata. Soft bottle brush flowers of lilac pink above a grassy foliage.

Lychnis chalcedonica—bright scarlet flattish heads, 3 feet high in June to August. L. viscaria is a grey-leaved plant with shocking pink campion flowers.

Lythrum. Loosestrife family. Yellow for the bog-side. There is L. salicaria Prichard's Variety which is pink.

Liliums—I recommend the purchase of a good lily catalogue to tell you of the various kinds. At times in this book I have advised the under-planting of shrubs with them. Some lilies do especially well in tubs and pots so they are very useful on tiny patios.

Monarda is the herb Bergamot. Cambridge Scarlet is red in July and August with weird honeysuckle like bearded flowers.

Nepeta. Cat-mint. N. Six Hills is 2 feet and has magnificent blue flowers and greyish foliage.

Oenothera is the well-known evening primrose—yellow convolvulous type flowers in June to August 2 feet. O. missouriensis has prostrate grey foliage and large flowers in June.

Papaver Orientalis. Huge oriental poppy flowers, red, pink or white $2\frac{1}{2}$ feet, June and July.

Paeonia. Get Messrs. Kelways Catalogue and have a mouth-drooling session with it. Then order some and enjoy their scent. It is subtle and sweet and full of nectar. The paeony needs no staking; you must leave it where it is as it resents disturbance, do not plant the crowns too deeply and make sure you order P. var. 'Jules Elie' which is a delicate silvery rose and fully double, and 'La France' which is pink double but showing delicate anthers of gold.

Phlox paniculatum. Require a rich loamy soil for these gloriously scented and coloured flowers—deep blue, mauve through pink and reds to white and cream—to delight you in July and August $2\frac{1}{2}$–3 feet high. Their enemy is eelworm.

Physostegia. Rose-coloured flowers in spires from August to September about 2 feet high.

Polygonatum multiflorum. 'Solomon's Seal', ideal for woodland planting.

Polygonum affine Donald Lowndes are small pink spires for ground cover. P. bissorta Superbum—has leaves very like a dock and large pink flowers at 3 feet in May and then on shorter stemmed ones for the rest of the season if dead-headed.

Potentilla. Gibson's Scarlet—a profusion of buttercup-like flowers with large strawberry type leaves all summer from June. Needs sun.

Pulmonaria is the Lungwort. It grows wild in Sussex where it is called Soldiers-Sailors, for the flowers are pink and blue. It flowers from March to May. P. rubra will flower soon after Christmas and is 9 inches high. P. azurea is 10 inches high and flowers the same time as the forsythia—so put some round the base of your bushes.

Salvia is of the sage family. I do have the variegated sage in my border. S. superba has many erect spikes of violet-blue 3–4 feet from June to August, and if you cut them back they will come again. S. Lubeca is a dwarf form, very rich in colour.

Sedums are ardent sun lovers and will bring as many butterflies to your garden as the buddleias do. Sedum 'Autumn Joy' has large flat-headed flowers of rich salmon-bronze about 18 inches high. S. 'Ruby Glow' is 9 inches high, and forms a spreading mat of red just when you need it, from August until October. S. spectabile 'Brilliant' is a glorious plant, about 1 foot in height, and makes a dense clump of magenta-pink flowers.

Sidalceas belong to the mallow family, and when I tell you that I had my first ones as a wedding present forty years

A view of
conifers and
heathers used
in association
in Adrian
Bloom's own
garden at
Bressingham,
Norfolk

ago, and I have moved some of them with me to and from four different gardens, you will realize they are fairly easy plants. S. 'Sussex Beauty' is pink and comes in June for many weeks, 3 feet tall. The ones I moved so much were S. 'Rosy Gem', S. 'Rose Queen' and S. 'Interlaken', though I have lost track by now of the ones that have survived.

Solidago is the golden rod, a much improved plant these days. 'Crown of Rays' is a good variety 18 inches high, good for small gardens with a primrose-coloured blooms.

Yucca filamentosa. An imposing plant. Good to use on its own on a terrace. It produces large groups of ivory white bells and has upright palm-like spiky foliage.

Zantedeschia 'Crowborough Variety' is an Arum Lily which grows freely in the open here in Sussex, but they need to be covered with straw or litter in more northerly climes. If you do not want to risk it in the open border you can sink it a foot deep in the pond and it will not be affected by the frost at all.

Heathers Now a word on heathers. Who can decide if they are small shrubs or perennial plants? They are generally low growing in habit, are excellent ground cover and have a flowering period of ten months or so.

Erica carnea 6–9 inches. Lime-tolerant.

King George has rose-pink flowers and dark green foliage December to February.

Erica carnea aurea has gold foliage—very bright in spring and summer.

Springwood White has bright green foliage, prostrate habit, and white flowers from January to March.

Calluna Vulgaris is the white heather from Scotland and needs an acid soil and clipping over in April.

C.v. Gold Haze is orange yellow. C.v. H. E. Beale has spikes of double rose-pink flowers.

Beoley Gold has bright golden foliage with sprays of white flowers from August to September.

The Cinerea varieties are the summer-flowering heathers who dislike lime at all costs. But they do like sun. They start flowering in June, go on until September, some into October. Erica cinerea 'Apple Blossom' has white flowers edged with pale pink, is 1 foot high and blooms from June to October. E.c. 'Atropurpurea' is a bright purple compact plant which blooms from June to September and is 8 inches high. E.c. 'Atrorubens' is red, and 9 inches high. E.c. 'Coccinea' is very dwarf with intense dark crimson flowers, 4 inches (good for the rockery) and flowers from June to September. E.c. 'Hookstone Lavender' and E.c. 'Hookstone White' have long spikes of flowers, 9 inches high, from June to October. E.c. 'John Eason' has copper foliage, 1 foot high, with deep pink flowers from June to September. E.c. 'Rosea Knaphill' variety has deep rose-pink flowers freely produced, 6 inches from June to October. E.c. 'Velvet Night' has very dark red flowers, 1 foot, June to September.

Erica hybrida darleyensis is early in December with purple-rose flowers, 18 inches high and goes on to April. E.h.d. 'Rubra' has mauve-purple flowers from February to April.

The Mediterranean varieties flower in the early spring and are bushy, upright and fairly tall. E.m. 'Hibernica' (syn, glauca) is pale pink, grows 3–4 feet high and flowers in March and April. E.m.c. 'Alba' is white, free-flowering and 2 feet. E.m.h. 'Rosea' is 2 feet and a clear pink. E.m.h. 'Silver Beads' is a white flowering, low growing, 18 inches heather, and flowers from January to April.

Erica vagans (the Cornish heath) is densely bushy, covering 3–4 feet of ground in time, and it flowers from July to August with long cylindrical spikes. E.v. 'Lyonesse' is pure white with chestnut anthers, is 2 feet high and blooms from July to October. E.v. 'Mrs D. F. Maxwell' is 2 feet and has deep cherry-pink flowers. E.v. 'St Keverne' is 2 feet and bright rose-pink.

Heathers are so much a country flower of the wide open spaces that purists might consider them quite out of place in a small garden. Do not let this deter you—they are hardy, colourful, flower over a long period, and are wonderful weed smotherers; but they must be used in groups of from four to seven and never less.

Bulbs In small gardens it is necessary to have as much show of flowers as possible and for this reason I often advise that there should be an underplanting of bulbs. One might divide the bulbs into three groups: A. The various daffodils and narcissii. B. The small species bulbs, such as snowdrops, crocus, species tulips, chionodoxas, grape hyacynths etc. and C. The summer bulbs, such as lilies of all kinds, alstroemarias, Nerine Bowdenii, gladiolus (especially the butterfly kinds), lily-of-the-valley, iris (rhizomes) Dahlias (tubers).

Dahlias. No plants have such a wealth of bloom or variety of colour as Dahlias—and they are so easy to grow—they are good in borders in groups, on their own in beds and will take the place of spring plants like tulips to prolong the season. There are several varieties—giant-flowered, decorative, cactus, pom-pom and coltness, with dwarf hybrids of various kinds. They range in colour from the darkest reds through rich purples and pale mauves, rust colours and bright orange-reds through to pale pinks, dark pinks and whites and creams.

Garden Chrysanthemums for autumn flowering are often purchased from the nurseryman in early summer, growing in peat pots, and are generally known as early flowering chrysanthemums. There are also Korean Chrysanthemums which are smaller, usually single-flowered and begin in August.

Chapter
8

Spotlight on some highlights

Featuring : Sundials. Statuary. Summerhouses.

You will always need focal points in parts of your garden; they may form centre pieces for a separate garden—they may indeed be there in the form of a well, or you may need to be reminded of your mortality by a sundial. These items like statuary, or pots on a terrace, are particularly valuable in the winter as items of interest to draw the eye from the bare earth and the bare branches and the mass of decaying foliage you have had to leave round your tender plants to preserve them from the frost. Indeed, if your urns and pots are of terracotta and your statues of marble, then they too will only catch the eye because they are hideously swathed in polythene and straw to keep out the frost!

But seriously . . . if you have divided your garden into several parts you will need a focal point in each. Terraces will need pots or troughs. A rose garden or a herb garden will need a bird bath or a sundial or an astrolabe, whilst a dovecote is best in a yard, midden or courtyard, so that the doves can sun themselves on roofs—preferably white doves against warm red and lichened tiles. Statuary is best against dark shrubs; yew will give the necessary old-time atmosphere.

Plants in pots or tubs or troughs will need constant attention. They will dry out very quickly to start with. They must never be allowed to look untidy, dead leaves must be removed, plants must be properly and discreetly staked, if on a windy site. Because you have drawn a lot of attention to the plants by putting them in pots you must make sure that they grow on without hindrance so that they are the best plants of their kind. Foliar feeding and liquid fertilisers must be constantly

applied, and, very important this, *never stand a pot or tub in a draught*. It is important that your pot or tub should conform with the rest of the house and terrace. If your house is Georgian, your pots must be also, ditto Victorian. Tubs are pretty ageless and can be used almost anywhere. I prefer them painted white, green being my second choice. Do not, I implore you, paint them blue or red or yellow—these are gay holiday Mediterranean colours, suitable for a holiday camp but not our sort of garden!

You can get all kinds of statuary at all kinds of prices and made of various materials. If you are very wealthy you can, and I hope you will, purchase an antique piece culled from some garden of yesteryear. It will set you back an awful lot, but the atmosphere it will give your garden will be beyond price. Site it well. The siting is almost as important as the statue you choose. Do not be afraid of a statue or garden ornament made of cement or re-constituted stone, because once weathered with moss and lichens they look very well indeed.

Dove-cotes are a delightful decoration for a garden. Do not be dissuaded because your garden is small, as there is no need to have live doves. A pair of china ones from Casa Pupo—the Spanish art shop in London or Brighton will do excellently.

Stone troughs are a fashionable ornament these days and a boon to the old, the invalid or the infirm. Stone sinks have been removed from kitchens to be replaced by steel or plastic ones—galvanised iron feeding troughs have replaced the stone ones on a farm and many a stone sink or trough is lying idle in some garden or farmyard corner. The idea of the trough is that in it you can grow the tiniest plants and know where they

Left:
A dovecote
used as a
feature in my
walled garden

are. Raised 3–4 feet off the ground the trough brings the miniature garden nearer to you without undue bending over or peering. It is, in short, a myopic's dream. You aim at a miniature garden within the bounds of your trough.

Sundials, bird baths are acceptable and should be chosen for their artistic proportions—and please, I beseech you, no gnomes or windmills.

Garden furniture should be chosen to last well. There are some very good replicas of old Victorian and Georgian garden furniture which although costly at first will last forever. White and green are good colours. A seat at the end of a walk is a good idea. You can use garden furniture, pots, vases, statuary as some focal point in your garden that gives the whole design an added meaning.

In a small paved area pots are seen to tremendous advantage. Strawberry pots are such a good way to grow strawberries where your space is small.

At the 1979 Chelsea Flower Show I realized that I should have to be on the premises, as it were, in the garden I designed (and from which incidentally I did three sound broadcasts every day for four days). What if it rains for four days? I thought. For this reason and for this reason alone I designed a trellis gazebo for the garden. I recorded the addresses of over 50 people who wanted to know where they could get one! So a summerhouse or shelter, or arbour, or porch is certainly a popular feature for a garden. Again, it is the placing of it in the design as perhaps the end of a journey that is important. A well-placed summerhouse incidentally is good screening for some feature of next door that you dislike. It's also an excellent addition of space upwards in a small garden, on which you can grow several roses, vines or clematis.

Centre: Pots full of herbs on a terrace are decorative and useful

This beautifully designed garden furniture is space saving and looks good on a patio

Chapter
9

Water for
a new dimension

Construction. Plants. Fish. Creating a fountain.

**Facing page:
The paved
garden I
designed for the
Chelsea Flower
Show in 1979,
with its pools
and gazebo
(see Plan 15 on
page 120)**

Water will add a completely new dimension to your garden,
be it a formal pond 2 feet square or a lake of several acres, it
provides another element, a complete change of scene and is
an added ornament to the whole garden. And remember, if
you are a lazy gardener (I'm sorry sir, I mean if you are a very
busy man!) then you will realize that an area of water does
not need weeding or mowing or digging, or pruning—indeed
the best thing to do with a pond is to lie down beside it and
peer into it, and contemplate what a wonderful new world of
life there is underneath that square of sun-lighted water.
Studying the natural history and the underwater life is a
wonderfully relaxing occupation. Joking aside though, there
is work to do of a kind. A pond does need understanding and
attention if it is to be a successful part of your garden.

If your pool is on a terrace or set in amongst paving, or if it
is to be part of a formal garden, it is better for it to be of
regular or geometric shape. Should you decide to have a pool
in some shady romantic spot as nature intended, it had better
be a naturally shaped pond.

There are, briefly, three ways of constructing a pool; you
can excavate a suitable hole to fit a prefabricated glass fibre
pool—preferably a geometrical shape rather than one like a
distorted kidney or other fancy shape. You can line your
excavated hole with butyl liner or your pond can be con-
structed of reinforced concrete. Butyl rubber rectangular pools
can be ordered prefabricated for single depth pools. Both
these ponds and the glass fibre ones can be filled with water at
once, plants and lilies established and the fish put in, but with

a concrete pool it is of the utmost importance that the water be changed several times over several weeks before the plants are well established. Several weeks after this you may then insert the fish. There are strong poisons and acids in cement which have to be soaked away before the fish can be well and happy. It is necessary for the plants to be established well enough for them to be giving off oxygen before the fish are introduced.

Select a level piece of ground, sited if possible in full sunshine and away from trees. The leaves in autumn fall into the pond and decay—the carbon dioxide gas given off by the decaying leaves will be bad for the fish and if the pond should be covered by ice for a time this gas will be unable to bubble to the surface and the fish will be killed. Excavate the earth, firming the remaining soil with a rammer and removing (if it is not to be a concrete pool) all stones and sharp protruding objects. If you are using a butyl liner cover the bottom with sand or sifted soil. Place the liner evenly over the excavation, stretched fairly tightly with stones, bricks, paving or passers-by distributed at regular intervals round the edge so that when you add the water the liner will immerse evenly. Start to fill slowly with water. The weight of the water will take the liner to the bottom of the pool and you will have left a large border of material to stay level round the top edge. You will need to leave a flap of about a foot to eighteen inches or so all round which will then be firmly and permanently held by paving slabs or stones placed formally and informally round the edge of the pool according to the shape you intend to achieve. The best effect is achieved if the stones overlap the edge of the pool by about two to three inches.

If the pool is to be of fibre glass make the hole the size and shape of the fibre glass pool you have bought, put in the pool, make sure it fits snugly and then put your slabs round the edge.

If the pool is to be a concrete one it is better to go to the expense of employing skilled labour to do this work to avoid the frustration of having a leaky pool. If however you do get cracks in a concrete pool these can be sealed by a plastic bituminous compound harmless to the plants and fish.

At the bottom of the pool put four inches of good loam and if this is covered with washed sand and gravel preferably taken from a swiftly running stream, then you will stand a better chance of clear water. Put in six inches of water, but do it slowly pouring it into a receptacle placed at the bottom of the pool so that you do not disturb the soil. If you are tempted to use manure for the waterlilies, as one is often advised to do, use very old cow manure which has been turned over several times over six months with the loam. The lily is then planted with its growing point just clear of the soil. May and June are the best months for this. Don't fill the pond completely but raise its level week by week as the waterlily leaves float on the surface. But the crowns must be covered with water immediately it is planted. If you need to thin pond plants out at any time May and June are the months to do it. Incidentally, the Arum lily is a good plant for pools so long as the crowns are well covered by the water in the winter; this way they are hardy and make an unusual display for a small pool. If your pond is already full and you want to plant a waterlily, lower it in a basket-type container and lower it week by week as the growth develops. Excellent for a large pool is Nymphaea virginalis which is the largest white-flowered waterlily. You can also choose yellow, cream, pink and red. N. masaniello is a rich carmine rose; N. Col. A. J. Welch is canary yellow for medium pools and there are also scented ones; be advised by an aquatic specialist.

As well as the waterlilies you must also have some submerged plants to give off oxygen, such as Ranunculus aquatilis (water crowsfoot), Vallsineria spiralis has long tape like leaves and with dark tufted foliage there is Ceratophyllum demersum (Hornwort). For the bank of a natural pool there is nothing nicer than some of the native wild plants like the Marsh Marigold (there is a double one too), the Water Mint and Water Forget-me-not, and then there is the glorious Yellow Flag Iris and Orange Loosestrife. Only use bullrushes in a large pool and then beware, they spread from seed like wildfire.

The most usual fish to keep are gold fish—but there are many colours, shapes and sizes—some with fantails, and there is the Shubunkin, a smooth goldfish with no scales. They breed easily and many will survive their cannibalistic cousins to populate the pool. Tench are dark-greenish black fish which stay near the bottom of the pool and are good scavengers and help to keep it well balanced. Water Snails are good for this

One of the pools in my Chelsea garden showing the Ali-baba pots as a decorative feature and fountain

91

too. My favourite fish are Golden or Silver Orfe—quicker and livelier than the goldfish and they often swim about in shoals.

Fish are moribund and inactive in the winter when they need no food. When you start your pond it is best to feed the fish with natural live food, like water fleas (Daphnia) and other minute aquatic insects, larvae, and tiny minute life like large bacteria called Infusoria—all of this can be obtained in cans from an aquatic supplier. If you use dried fish food, please give them only as much as they will eat at once—otherwise it decays in the pond and causes disease.

If your pond gets very green rake the algae, that is, the green slime, off the surface of the pond a few times. Green water is usually caused by too much sunshine on a newly established pond. As the waterlilies begin to shade the water with their growing leaves and the other plants get well established you will find that the whole pond will become 'balanced', the water will clear and all the inhabitants, that is, plants, fish, insects, snails etc., will begin to play their part as nature intended and all will clear and settle in.

Keep a ball or a log bouncing on the surface of the pond in winter and it will dissuade ice from forming and, when removed, will enable you to lever some ice out. Do not hammer the ice to break it—it will concuss the fish. The hot base of a kettle of boiling water will make a hole in the ice. It is bad to let ice cover the pond for too long as it seals in the gasses of decaying leaves and stops the fish getting their absolutely necessary supply of oxygen.

The best fountains are motored with fountain pumps which feature an electric motor sealed into a plastic block to keep the water from it and to insulate it electrically. These can be bought for both fountains and waterfalls. I strongly advise the fitting of the items by an experienced electrician as water and electricity can be very dangerous companions especially when children and pets are about. This is a job for a fully qualified expert.

Fountains do complete a pool and are so cool sounding on a very hot day. Site your fountain where light will play on it. It is the effect of light on the water which gives the greatest pleasure. Don't plant your lilies immediately under a fountain as the constant dripping may inhibit the growth—that is if you are going to have the fountain playing for long periods.

The reflection of the sun and the sky on the water, all its teeming life and the lively playing of the fountain's jets of water add a great deal to a small garden. The mystery of the myriad forms of life will amaze and delight you. I feel in the same way that a house is not a home without welcoming dogs and a log fire to smile rosily at you in winter, so a garden is incomplete without the element of water with all its added beauty.

A weeping pear
(Pyrus
salicifolia
pendula) is
preferable to a
weeping willow
in a small
garden and
looks very good
by a pool

Chapter
10

Designs on your garden

15 plans for small gardens, each accompanied by a description and list of plants used.

Facing page:
At the 1980
Chelsea Flower
Show

The following pages show a series of suggestions on how to deal with variously shaped gardens. It does not follow that your garden can possibly be of the same dimensions, shape or aspect; but you could choose a little from one plan and a little from the other according to your own particular site (or dilemma!).

All walls need to be clothed and the following plants can be used—Jasmine (summer and winter), Wisteria, Honeysuckle, Roses, Clematis, Ivies (Hedera), various vines, be they for fruit or foliage or both, Cherries, Plums, Apricots, Apples Peaches, Pears, Hydrangea, Passion flowers, Pyracantha Cotoneaster, Cydonia, Ceanothus, Magnolia Grandiflora, Garrya elliptica, Escallonia langleyensis.

All paths will need small low plants and shrubs planted here and there and the following are suggestions—Achillea argentea, A. tomentosa, Alyssum montanum, Armeria (Thrift), Aubrieta (various), Campanula (various), Bellium minutum (false daisy), Dianthus (various), Heathers (Ericas) various Helianthemum (Sun roses various), Sedum (Stonecrop various), Hypericum nummularium, Mentha requienni (Mint), Saxifraga various, Thymus Serpyllum, Sagina Glabra and small Glauca Hebes (various).

The shapes are here and I have also suggested various plantings. If you refer to and consult Chapters V, VI and VII you will find there all the trees, shrubs and plants that you will require for any small garden and you can decide for yourself instead of accepting my suggestions. Make changes especially if your soil or aspect demand it.

PLAN 1: A triangular garden

As you leave the house you step out onto a circular or semi-circular raised patio of York paving, or similar type paving. This has two steps about 2 feet wide and 9 inches in depth to lawn X and similar steps upwards to lawn Y. At the corner of the house there is a pond.

Between the two steps down and the two steps up i.e. between 3 and 5 is one level area the width of the 2 steps and the same level as the raised patio. On this there should be a long garden seat.

At the end of lower lawn X in the corner is a gazebo of lattice covered with climbing roses 'Zephirine Drouhin' and Clematis 'Vyvyan Pennell'. The pink of the one contrasted nicely with the pale blue double flowers of the other. There will be matching York paving as floor to the gazebo with 9-inch step up from the lawn semi-circular to match the terrace.

The garden is fenced with ranch-type fencing, on which there are espalier fruit trees and cordon apple trees at intervals.

In the apex corner of the upper lawn there is a group of conifers backed with Chamaecyparis lawsoniana 'Erecta' and with C.l. 'Stewartii' and C.l. 'Lutea' in front with several bushes of Philadelphus coronarius 'Aureus' plus two bushes of Juniperus virginiana 'Grey Owl' to edge of grass.

The beds A on the front of the house are to contain a selection of perennial plants, such as Agapanthus, Hostas etc. with Hydrangea petiolaris (the climbing hydrangea) and Wisteria sinensis to climb the house wall, and bulbs etc. to fill in.

The pond will have Iris variegata at its edges with water lilies and other aquatic plants according to your taste.

Opposite the corner of the house and to mask the different levels will be a planting of 2 poplar trees—Populus × candicans 'Aurora', which has variegated green, white and pink leaves in the spring, and the balsam poplar which has a glorious perfume in the spring; Populus balsamifera. Spaced amongst the two poplars will be Picea pungens 'Moerheimii', a very blue spruce. Cryptomeria japonica 'Elegans' and Chamaecyparis pisifera 'Squarrosa Sulpherea' with two or three plants of Juniperus squamata 'Meyeri' to camouflage the edges of the terrace steps.

The steps to be edged with Lavendula 'Hidcote' and the paving and steps to be dotted here and there with paving plants.

1. Picea pungens 'Moerheimii'
2. Chamaecyparis pisifera 'Squarrosa Sulphurea'
3. Populus × candicans 'Aurora'
4. Cryptomeria japonica 'Elegans'
5. Populus balsamifera
6. Juniperus squamata 'Meyeri'

PLAN 2: Oblong town garden

As you leave the house you step out onto a small paved terrace of simulated York paving or concrete slabs, each slab 2 feet square. Down two steps of 1 foot 6 inches width and 9 inch risers onto either a grass lawn or cobbled area (perhaps paved with granite sets or with bricks in particular patterns) in which paving slabs are set at intervals of the same size and material as the terrace. The smaller squares are also paving of the same material but 1 foot square.

On the right as you descend the steps is a bed containing silver and dark green plants in a pattern and on the left of the terrace before you descend is a raised bed the same height as the terrace. This is planted with a colour scheme of blue and dark mahogany and purple.

As you progress along the paving slabs on the left is a spreading blue juniper shrub and at the end of the path a golden coniferous tree, behind which is a pond. This pond is backed by a wall made of pierced concrete slabs. In the corner (11) is a bush of feathery maple over the edge of the pond and climbing roses 'Albertine' and 'Park Direktor Riggers' are grown. The reason for choosing the two is to extend the growing season.

The flagged path then leads into a small area where there are household bins, compost heap, and a small shed. Opposite the end of the path and climbing the fence here is the large leaved variegated ivy (Hedera canariensis Variegata). The long bed (7) contains 3 cordon apples.

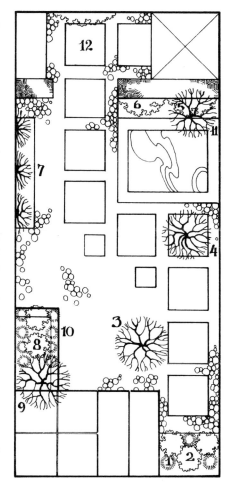

1. Helichrysum augustifolium
2. Chamaecyparis pisifera 'Nana'
3. Juniperus suamata Meyeri
4. Chamaecyparis lawsoniana stewartii, in bed 2 feet square
5 & 6. Roses 'Albertine' and 'Park Direktor Riggers'
7. 3 Cordon apples
8. Phorium Tenax Purpureum (2 plants)
9. Juniperus sabina 'Blue Danube'
10. Erica carnea atropurpureum (interplanted with gladiolus Byzantinus)
11. Acer palmatum dissectum variegatum
12. Hedera canariensis variegata

PLAN 3: Tiny paved garden

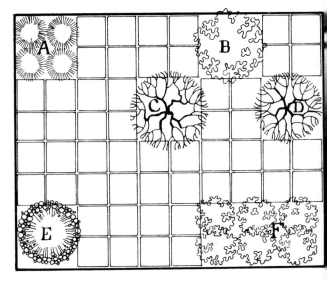

Here we have little more than a paved area with an occasional few pavings removed for planting.

What is needed is a group of similar plants, such as Avena candida, which is a blue grey hummocky grass—or Festuca ovina glauca, which is shorter and bluer. Hakonechlora is a golden-leaved grass but it dies back between November and March.

Dwarf conifers are suitable furnishings too—Thuja orientalis 'Rosedalis' changes colour seasonally and only grows to 3 feet high. In winter it is purple-brown, in spring, butter-yellow and in summer, light green. Thuja occidentalis 'Rheingold' is also useful—it is conical and grows to 12 feet eventually—but is very slow growing. Pinus mugo Gnom is dark green and compact. Juniperus squamata 'Blue Star' makes a dense bush of steel blue and is excellent.

Other useful shrubs for these small paved areas are Senecio laxifolius (grey or silver), Santolina in various forms, also silver, and Fatsia japonica, which is evergreen and has leaves 'like a nine-fingered hand', which are a shiny deep green. This is how Christopher Lloyd describes them in *Foliage Plants* published by Collins. F.j. Variegata is splashed with white. It grows well in shade and will eventually grow too large for a small area. Yuccas are good architectural plants to use in paved beds.

Plants can include most of the dianthus, variegated thyme, and variegated sage. Miniature roses are useful. If you have a damp, dark area then ferns can be used, a very beautiful one being the evergreen Polystichum setiferum Acutilobum. Iris germanica of various colours always look well with paving. Hostas are good for paved beds.

If they were not so unsightly, hideously stark as they are in their nasty plastic coverings, too, tom-bags or 'Grow-bags' are an excellent addition to a small paved garden area; the extra heat coming up from the paving in a small sheltered area helping greatly the ripening of tomatoes. I have suggested to the manufacturers that they should have green pictures of trailing plants printed on the bags to make them more acceptable to the aesthetically minded, but to no avail. However, you can mask the sides with brick or stone curbs for edging and fill in to cover the bag with a little extra peat or ICI composted bark and immediately they marry in more happily.

A. Avena candida
B. Fatsia japonica
C. Thuja occidentalis 'Rheingold'
D. Juniperus squamata 'Blue Star'
E. Senecio laxifolius
F. Roses. 'Royal Salute' a dwarf rose from John Mattocks, underplanted with Tulipa gregii

PLAN 4: Tiny L-shaped courtyard

This is a small space 14 feet × 14 feet at its longest dimensions. You step out of the door onto a series of concrete or simulated stone circular flags F; if the site is uneven these could be overlapping stepping stones of full circle, but I visualise them as being of one level and cemented together with a surround of cobble stones set in mortar on a concrete base. The largest circle being 3 feet in diameter. At the edges of the circles as they meet each other and the cobbling, small pockets may be left to fill with earth for such small plants as alyssum, aubrieta, thyme, campanula, perennial candytuft and other mat forming plants and shrubs. This path leads round to C which is a flat—almost on the ground—circular vase also 3 feet in diameter. This can be kept as a birdbath with water in it or it can be planted in spring with small species tulips, crocus, snowdrops, muscari etc. with polyanthus or primroses to give the arrangement body. All this would be removed for a summer display of Helichrysum petiolatum (a silver, felt-leaved, spreading plant) with perhaps three pelargoniums of my favourite Lord Bute with Viola cornuta climbing under and over and through the other plants. A is a semi-circular bed containing a Yucca gloriosa and B is of similar size containing a very blue and also very slow-growing Picea pungens Globosa. D is a large bed. To the centre of the bed so that it will spread well is Juniperus × media 'Old Gold'. Purchase your plant at a garden centre so that you can choose one

to spread both left, right and forward. Behind it in the corner and to spread on both sides of the wall or fence is Pyracantha 'Orange Charmer'. Underplant this bed with daffodils for the spring show Bed E is furnished with the giant Euphorbia wulfenii interplanted with bulbs of Galtonia candicans to lengthen the season.

A. Yucca gloriosa
B. Picea pungens Globosa
C. The low vase to contain spring: bulbs and polyanthus summer: Helichrysum petiolatum. Pelargonium 'Lord Bute' Viola cornuta
D. Juniperus × media 'Old Gold'. Pyracantha 'Orange Charmer'. Daffodils
E. Euphorbia wulfenii. Galtonia candicans

PLAN 5: The long, sloping garden

Terracing and slope with curves to shorten in effect a long narrow site on three levels. Site is $25\frac{1}{2}$ feet × $58\frac{1}{2}$ feet.

The whole garden is fenced with ranch-type fencing. The paving is all of York stone, or of artificial York stone of a neutral shade. One steps out of the French windows onto a curved terrace of paving which is on the same level as grass and shrubbery border (P and P). To the left near the house is a collection of slow growing Juniperus squamata Meyeri and Juniperus virginiana 'Grey Owl' in front with Juniperus virginiana burkii and with Chamaecyparis pisifera 'Squarrosa Sulphurea', and Thuja occidentalis 'Lutea Nana' in the middle at the back—a phalanx of 3 and a bit squashed in with only 12 feet or so and a bit near the house foundations! If there is room in front, with one or two bushes of mop head hydrangea in pink.

The two beds F_1 and F_2 are on either side of the house and extend round the edges of the circular paving—approximately 3 feet wide.

In the right-hand corner is planted a Cedrus atlantica Glauca on the same level as the terrace A (too big a species for this part of the garden eventually but very decorative for the first twenty years!).

These borders, as they are near the house, should be interplanted with daffodils and narcissus for the spring and lilies for the summer.

Down split circular and semi-circular steps one goes down 2 feet to a large circular lawn 22 feet or so in diameter with a flower border around it of about a foot in width. It is backed by a low retaining dry wall of York stone 2 feet high. Below it the flower border will contain a selection of choisya ternata, agapanthus, dwarf philadelphus, kurume azalea Palestrina, cistus and brooms. (In season planted with pink lily flowered tulips. When these circular borders lose the protection of the retaining wall and become borders F these will be planted with various different colour flowered and foliaged heathers.

There is grass in Area Z with a planting of spring bulbs and in the space to the right 20 there is a small cherry surrounded by the dark foliage of osmanthus bushes.

The third circle is of York paving and is reached down similar steps and is 1 foot lower. In the centre of the paving is pond and in the corner a silver weeping pear Pyrus salcifolia Pendula. The fence between Y and the tree is covered with Rosa filipes 'Kiftsgate'—a very vigorous white scented rose.

Area M is for fruit trees—cordon and espalier and a selection of decorative vegetables.

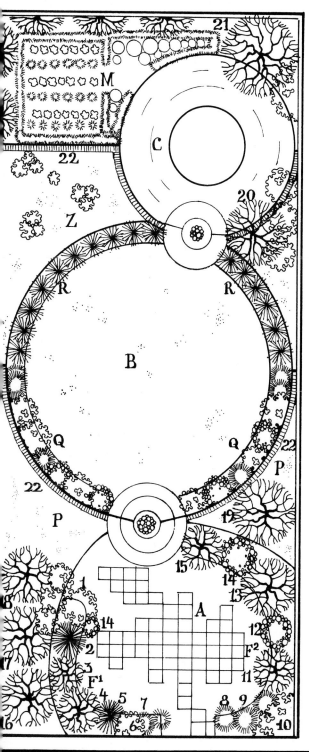

A. Paved patio area—large York stone paving slabs
B. Grass roundel
C. Paving circular area with pond in centre

All the above areas to be connected with steps

In Space F₁

1. Skimmia japonica rubella
2. Berberis thunbergii Atropurpurea Nana
3. Picea pungens globosa
4. Acer palmatum Dissectum
5. Viburnum tinus
6. Wisteria sinensis (growing up house wall)
7. Group of dwarf evergreen azaleas

In Space F₂

8. Group of dwarf evergreen azaleas
9. Group of dwarf evergreen azaleas
10. Magnolia grandiflora (attached to house wall)
11. Acer palmatum Dissectum Atropurpurea
12. Senecio laxifolius greyii
13. Juniperus communis Depressa Aurea
14. Clumps of Iris Germanica
15. Juniperus Boulevard

In Space P

16.
17. Conifers fronted by hydrangea
18.
19. Cedrus Atlantica Glauca

Flower borders Q
Clumps of choisya ternata, agapanthus, dwarf syringa, kurume azalea Palestrina, cistus and brooms.

20. Group of cherry tree surrounded by bushes of osmanthus
21. Pyrus salcifolia Pendula
22. Hedge of lavender

Flower borders R
Low-growing heathers of various colours and foliage.

M. Fruit trees and vegetables

PLAN 6: Serpentine herbaceous border garden

This garden might be at its best surrounded by a brick wall. At the end of the border we must have a focal point, be it a seat, a statue—perhaps a pond surrounded by a Yew hedge. A dove-cote standing in a smothering of herbs. In my design I have two short lengths of Yew hedge coming at right angles from the walls on the left and at the bottom of the garden. Each about 6 feet high and a pillar of yew with a topiary ball at the top of each as a finial of 8 feet high to end each length of hedge, thus forming an architectural entrance. Inside will be the gazebo or whatever.

The garden is simplicity itself and will need a keen gardener to tend it and nurture it, and make it look like a haphazard exuberance of bloom through as long a season as possible.

The path is to be of crazy paved stone of the local area and to contain, especially from the edges, as many rock plants, herbs and other low growing perennials as possible—the edges of the walk will thus be blurred with colour and a contrived difference in texture of foliage of the tiny plants spilling over beneath our feet if we are not careful as we walk.

Leaving the house by the door on the left hand house wall is a clematis Barbara Jackman (blue), Then on the left hand wall at the back of the border is a Cydonia japonica or orange-flowering Quince, then comes climbing rose Etoile de Holland, then Clematis Montana, then a large space of many feet taken by the Russian Vine (Polygonum baldschuanicum). Then comes the Yew enclosure and along the bottom wall we have Vitis vinifera purpurea a purple vine). Then the ordinary common dark ivy with variegated ivy (Hedera helix Buttercup) beginning the next side wall, followed by the climbing Hydrangea petiolaris, then there is an espalier peach tree, then the 'Albertine' rose, followed by Rosa virgiana plena, which is also on the house wall mingling if you like with a Wisteria. On the right is the list of shrubs and herbaceous plants used in the borders, commencing with the right hand border.

I am, of course, aware of the fact that many experts will consider this garden very old-fashioned; especially in the amount of work which will have to be expended on it and the fact that the garden will do little for its owner in the late autumn and early spring; but the season can be extended with the interplanting of bulbs of all kinds and it is the garden for the enthusiast who has endless time and only a small garden. Ask me to come and see it!

1. Acanthus mollis
2. Kolkwitzia amabilis (2 bushes)
3. Pyrus salicifolia pendula
4. Chamaecyparis pisifera 'Boulevard'
5. Chamaecyparis 'Lutea'
6. Rose 'Iceberg'
7. Berberis thunbergii Atropurpurea Nana
8. Paeonia lutea (Yellow tree paeony)
9. Hosta sieboldiana Elegans (bluish foliage)
10. ⎫
11. ⎬ A wide spread of heather with yellow foliage —you choose
12. ⎭
13. Aster frikarti
14. Weigela florida variegata
15. Iris germanica —Queechee, rich garnet red
16. Senecio cineraria 'White Diamond'. (This is to be treated as an annual or a perennial according to your climate c the severity of the winter!)
17. Phalaris arundinacea variegata
18. Stachys lanata (Lambs lugs)
19. Lychnis chalcedonia
20. Achillea Gold Plate
21. Pieris 'Wakehurst'

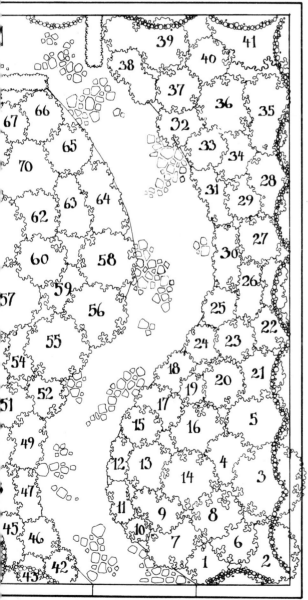

22. Heliopsis 'Golden Plume'
23. Sidalcea 'Rose Queen'
24. Salvia superba
25. Spanish Gorse (Genista hispanica)
26. Campanula allieriaefolia (white)
27. Rose chinensis 'Old Blush'
28. Genista aetnensis
29. Monarda 'Cambridge Scarlet'
30. Stokesia 'Blue Star'
31. Iris pallida variegata
32. Alchemilla mollis
33. Group of red lupins
34. Miscanthus japonicus variegatum
35. Viburnum tomentosum Mariesii
36. Aster Harringtons Pink
37. Tree Paeony, Paeonia × lemonei 'Alice Harding'
38. Artemesia Lambrook Silver
39. Euphorbia wulfenii
40. Arundinaria viridistrata
41. Olearia macrodonta
42. Pulmonaria
43. Paeonia suffruticosa 'Renkaku' (double-white)
44. Cotinus coggygria 'Royal Purple'
45. Delphinium 'Giant Pacific Summer Skies'
46. Libertia
47. Hosta sieboldiana 'Elegans'
48. Philadelphus Coronarius Aureus
49. Alchemilla mollis
50. Aruncus sylvestre
51. Campanula lactifolia
52. Avena candida (Blue Grass)
53. Thalictrum angustifolium
54. Phlox paniculata 'Starfire'
55. Acer dissectum 'Variegatum'
56. Yucca filamentosa
57. Euphorbia wulfenii
58. Alchemilla mollis
59. Veronica 'Blue Fountain'
60. Phormium tenax—the copper variety
61. Acer negundo variegatum as a tree
62. Sedum Autumn Joy
63. Nepeta grandiflora 'Blue Beauty'
64. A drift of pinks (Dianthus). You choose
65. Erigeron 'Prosperity'
66. Anaphalis yedoensis
67. Delphinium 'Black Knight'
68. Sambucus nigra 'Aurea'
69. Chamaecyparis lawsoniana 'Pembury Blue'
70. Heliopsis 'Golden Plume'

PLAN 7: The basement garden

This is a very small garden—almost a basement area—8½ feet × 16 feet. You leave the house to descend 2½ feet by brick, or stone, steps to a level area D. On your right is a built-up bed B with retaining walls 2½ feet high. This level area D also contains an area marked C which is of the same level and is marked off with a brick curb. This triangular bed can be of earth and contain the sunny foliaged small tree Gleditsia triacanthos 'Sunburst', or it can be used as a pond or a sandpit for junior.

At the other end of the paved area D are some steps up to the exit gate on the left of which is another bed contained by a retaining wall 2½ feet high. Bed A.

The area D can be paved with York paving, real or simulated, or could also be of brick. The garden walls surrounding the area are 5 feet high and this is the reason for raising the beds to get them as much light as possible. It is a fairly open site and plants have not been chosen especially for shade.

Various climbing plants are used for the house and surrounding walls.

If C is kept as a bed for low growing plants e.g. Aubrieta and Iberis, they can be grown with spring bulbs amongst them. Autumn Crocus is also a suggestion.

There are three groups of pots one on each step and a group on the pavement under bed A. One group could well be strawberry pots. Another could have Pelargoniums and some could be house plants (Azalea Indica brought out for the summer months only.

Ferns could be grown in crevices of the walls and where the paving meets the walls.

In the group of steps leading to the gate, so that they will be seen from the house, a plant of Cotoneaster horizontalis perpusillus (a very dwarf variety) could be planted and trained along each step riser. House leeks may be grown on the top of the retaining walls.

Other wall plants to grow from Area D up the outside walls could include variegated Ivy, Climbing Hydrangea, roses clematis and even a small espalier peach!

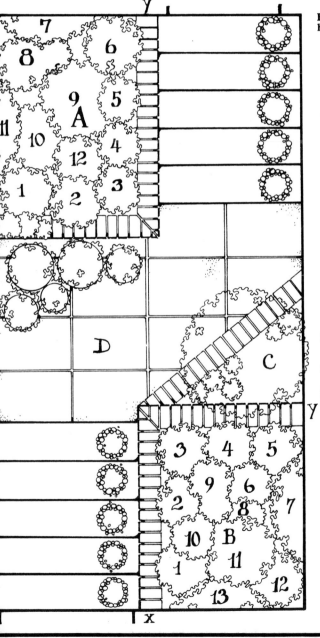

Bed B nearest the house

1. Nepeta grandiflora 'Blue Beauty'
2. Geranium macrorrhizium (leaves smell of sweet briar)
3. Stachys lanata (Lambs lugs)
4. Aster frikarti
5. Hebe 'Albicans'
6. Monarda
7. Jasminum nudiflorum (To be trained up and along wall. The yellow winter flowering one.)
8. Anaphalis margaritacea (Grey leaves and heads good for drying and using in flower arrangement.)
9. Anthemis 'Thora Perry'
10. Polygonum bisorta 'Superbum'
11. Mahonia japonica (shrub)
12. Acanthus mollis
13. Rose to climb up the house. I would like to suggest 'Mermaid' as it is delicate, single yellow and will not be too vigorous.

Bed A

1. Sedum 'Ruby Glow'
2. Genista hispanica
3. Clump of Chives
4. Dianthus (Mrs Sinkins is a white one)
5. Erigeron Foersters Liebling (red)
6. Rosemarinus procumbans
7. Jasminum officinale 'Affine' (scented climber)
8. Achillea 'Gold Plate'
9. Acer palmatum dissectum atropurpureum
10. Picea pungens prostrata
11. Wisteria sinensis (for up and along the wall)
12. Hosta crispula

Bed C

Gleditsia triacanthos 'Sunburst'
Aubrieta
Iberis
Autumn Crocus

PLAN 8: Long, narrow, level garden

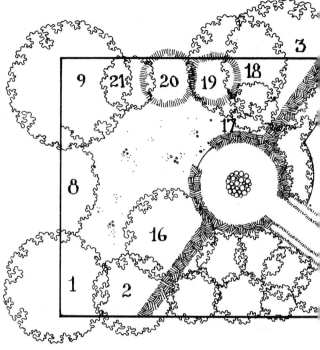

This is a long narrow level site which I have treated with straight lines to get away from the usual oblong look. There is a brick terrace for sitting out and on the house wall either side of the door are Wisteria sinensis and a climbing rose—either 'Golden Showers', which climbs up to about 9 feet, or 'Gloire de Dijon', which is an old rose of proven charm and might suit this garden well as its low box hedges and yew hedge (to hide the second half) do give the garden an old-fashioned atmosphere. On the fences either side of the terrace are Hydrangea petiolaris and the well-known 'Albertine' rose.

The terrace is separated by a low box hedge of about $1\frac{1}{2}$ feet high and on the left of a brick herringbone path is a triangular shrubbery. This contains plants to flower through the season and is interplanted with daffodils and narcissus for the spring and Lilium regale—gloriously scented lilies for later in the season. A clump or two of nerines might be added for the autumn if you live in a sheltered area south of the Trent.

On the fence backing this shrubbery is a pink rose 'Queen of Denmark', which has a long-flowering period.

On the right is a lawn with a pond in the centre, the pond being optional as this is not a large grass area and it could look fussy; but a pond does give continuous interest. It is bordered with York stone pavings

and can have a fountain if desired, water lilies etc. At the back of the border there are climbing roses, ivy, jasmine (winter and/or summer) as desired. The border is largely for herbaceous plants and I give a list of suggested ones. Here and there to give it more permanence and to save labour you could plant a group of 3 evergreen azaleas, and a broom or two. Plant the Acanthus in a corner to give strength to the arrangement and contrive to have brightly coloured flowers against the darkness of the Yew.

A second triangular bed on the left of the path is filled behind its box hedge with old-fashioned shrub and species roses with 'Goldfinch' and 'Maigold' growing on the fence. I give six other

1. Amelanchier
2. Robinia hillieri
3. Prunus cerasifera Pissardii (purple-leaved plum)
4. Rose 'Albertine'
5. Wisteria sinensis
6. Rose 'Golden Showers' or 'Gloire de Dijon'
7. Hydrangea petiolaris
8. Prunus Serrulata Yukon (pale primrose-yellow)
9. Mulberry Tree (Morus nigra)
10. Berberis stenophylla
11. Viburnum opulus compactum
12. Rhus typhina. Stag's Horn Sumach

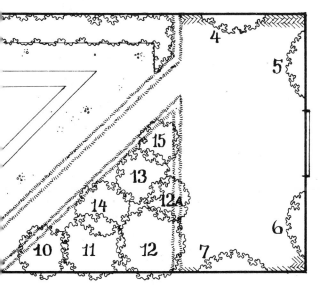

suggestions but go to somewhere like Sissinghurst in late June and you can choose the ones that please you.

We now come to the real feature of the garden, which is the Yew hedge, drawn diagonally with a roundel effect to pass through. I suggest a height of 6 feet to 6 feet 6 inches for this and as the garden is small we must keep the hedge trimmed well as to width as the diameter of the circle is but 7 feet approximately. Inside is a cobbled circle in the brick pavement.

As we come out on the other side we have a miniature grassy dell—only 15 feet × 8 feet or so—and for this reason the trees and shrubs chosen are small. Crocus, snowdrops, bluebells, scillas, muscaris, are amongst the shrubs together with some bulbs of Galtonia candicans—which is like an enormous snowdrop that flowers in July. Fritillaria and primroses too—and a few Gladiolus primulinus for later on.

I've included a Mulberry to harmonise with the Yew and the box and the old-fashioned roses in period. It will grow slowly but it is an interesting tree, with its dark loganberry like fruit when the tree gets a little older. And when it is a little older you could throw the garland ribbons of a Rosa filipes 'Kiftsgate' right through its topmost branches.

2a. Fuchsia tricolour (hardy)
3. Rose 'Iceberg'
4. Camellia 'Donation'
5. Santolina
6. Acer griseum
7. Berberis darwinii
8. Malus Profusion
9. Ilex aquifolium argenteo marginata elegantissimo
10. Pieris formosa forrestii 'Wakehurst'
11. Buddleia alternifolia (pink and trailing)

Old Roses
Rose Blanc Double de Coubert (rugosa)
Lavender Lassie (mauve/blue)
Hunter (dark red)
Golden Moss (yellow moss rose)
Magenta (musk rose)
Rosa Mundi (deep pink splashed with white)

Growing on fence
Goldfinch and Maigold

Some suggestions for the flower border
Acanthus spinosa (in corner)
Penstemon 'George Home' (hardy)
Aquilegia
Bergenia
Philadelphus coronarius aureus
Stachys lanata
Helleborus niger
Galega
Gloriosa Daisies
Group of Hemerocallis lilies
Hosta undulata medio-variegata
Hosta sieboldiane Elegans
Groups of dianthus of all kinds for front
Nepeta mussonii
Echinops ritro
Campanula latifolia
Campanula Glomerata superba
Aster frikartii
Artemisia 'Lambrook Silver'

PLAN 9: The wide garden

This site is fairly large being 18 yards × 12 yards. As you enter the garden from the house there is a York stone terrace with two shaped beds D and E. These are edged with low box hedges (1 foot high) and contain a selection of perhaps 4 shrub roses of the old-fashioned kind. (See Chapter VII.) Along the edge of the terrace, which is 9 inches higher than the grass lawn and herbaceous borders, are six topiary yews about 4/5 feet high. (A on the plan.)

Some semi-circular steps take us 3 feet 3 inches down from the terrace (2 feet 6 inches lower than the grass) into a semi-circular fan-shaped sunken garden. The first two steps are cut out of the upper terrace in semi-circular form. Then the next level is a circle and the next level is that of the sunken garden where the paths are either of the same York stone or very old brick. The steps being about 2 feet wide (diameter of the circular landing is 6 feet) and the risers being approximately 10 inches high. There are fan rose beds with narrow paths between them (R), each bed to contain hybrid tea roses. It might be preferable for one variety in each bed. All fragrant please!

A suggested arrangement might be R_1 'Duke of Windsor', which is bright vermilion, R_2 'Sutters Gold' yellow, R_3 'Prima Ballerina' deep pink and R_4 'Ernest H. Morse' a good strong red, but 'Papa Meilland' for a dark velvety red. If you are allergic to a very bright, light red rose then the 'Duke of Windsor' might be changed to a glorious white rose 'Pascali'.

The edge of the top of the retaining wall round the sunken garden should have a low hedge of 'Hidcote' lavender.

The beds marked H are for herbaceous plants, the corners B and C being either a group of variously coloured conifers for winter effect, or small trees, such as cherries, robinias, amelanchiers, acers etc. To fill the beds consult the herbaceous section of Chapter VII.

A quirky idea for the centre of each of the herbaceous borders in front of the conifers and spreading either side might be to plant a selection of spiky spear-shaped plants, such as the following: Phormium Tenax or Yucca filimentosa at the back and Iris germanica, Iris pallida variegata, Gladioli, Montbretia Crocosmia, Avena candida (blue grass) and Festuca glauca in the foreground. You could brighten the group with Phalaris arundinacea Picta (Gardeners' Garters) or Hakonechlora macro-alba aurea variegata (learn the name off by heart to impress your friends).

As a focal point between the two herbaceous beds, which are surrounded by yew hedges, is a shaped yew hedge standing on its own 9 feet wide by 9 feet high at its peak and perhaps 6 feet high at the sides. Standing freely in front of this is a statue, or a sundial, on a square of York paving if you prefer, or just on the lawn.

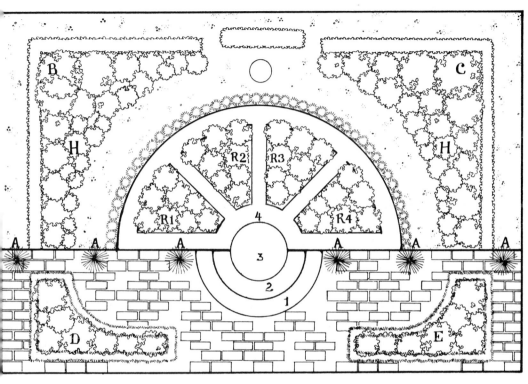

HOUSE

A. Topiary yews
B Various
& coloured
C. conifers or
   small trees e.g.
   cherries,
   robinias,
   amelianchers,
   acers.
D Old-fashioned
& shrub
E roses
H Herbaceous
   plants
R Hybrid tea
   roses

PLAN 10: Terrace house garden

The dimensions of this site are very challenging. We have a space 12 feet × 23 feet 6 inches surrounded by a foot-thick wall.

The end by the house is higher than the end by the gate and it has been decided to have a level terrace of 6 feet × 12 feet as a brick paved area. This is connected to the lower garden by three steps with 1½ feet treads and each step rising by 8 inches. Thus the lower garden is 2 feet below the terrace. The terrace is edged by a wall 3 feet high.

To the right of the steps is a circular pond edged in brick which is 5 feet 6 inches in diameter. From the wall, through a lead lion head fountain, water runs into the pond. To the left of the pond and filling largely the remaining part of the garden is another brick area, 7 feet in diameter. This is joined to the steps by an irregular-shaped brick paved space to the right of which is a terracotta vase of the Alibaba type for strawberries, which ends the sloping retaining wall of the steps. This piece of brick paved space has small cushion plants here and there. The other end of the brick circle is connected to the gate by a curved brick path. The remaining areas are earth beds. The walls are covered in climbing plants at intervals; starting on the left-hand side a Climbing Hydrangea is partly on the house and partly on the wall surround. Down this left-hand wall are climbing roses with clematis in each bed to prolong the period of flower; also there is a Ceanothus 'Cascade' which is evergreen.

At the end of the brick paving and at the side of the circular paved area is a bed containing herbaceous plants (various to be decided by personal choice of the gardener). In the bottom left-hand corner is the bright sunlight of evergold Chamaecyparis lawsoniana Erecta Aurea fronted by a Senecio laxifolius greyii and beside a Prunus cyclamina—a small flowering cherry with pink blossom and coppery foliage. The base of this tree is planted with golden heathers in variety. Between the curved brick path and the pond is another space containing first of all Juniperus communis depressa Aurea, then a weeping silver pear Pyrus salicifolia and between this in the tiny triangular space between pond and wall is Acer dissectum Atropurpureum. In the next triangular space between the wall and the retaining wall of the terrace is a clump of Iris germanica, which is interplanted with gladiolus to give a longer flowering period. There is also an Ivy here—silver and self clinging to spread up the retaining wall Hedera helix Glacier. By the house door is a bush of Rosemary to fondle as you go in and out, with climbing rose and clematis in the corner. May I suggest 'Maigold', semi-double, very fragrant blooms of bronze yellow (repeat flowering) with clematis tangutica with rich yellow lantern like flowers in autumn. There are waterlilies in the pool, together with goldfish. If your pond is 2 feet deep you can keep 6 fish of approximately 6 inches long.

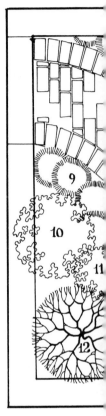

1. Climbing hydrangea up wall and up house wall
2. Climbing rose and clematis
3. Clematis Montana—this to go up both the garden wall and the retaining wall
4. Climbing rose and clematis
4a. Rosemary
5. Clump of Iris Germanica interplanted with Gladiolus

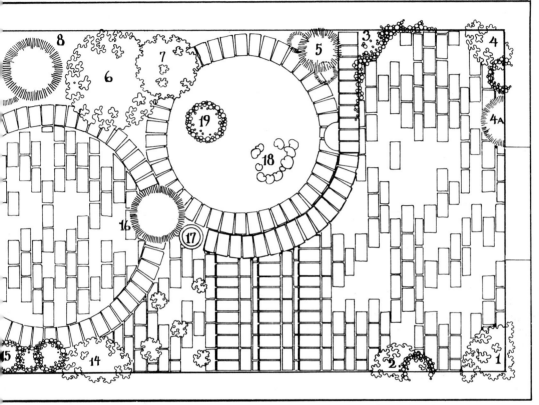

6. Weeping silver pear. Pyrus salcifolia pendula
7. Acer dissectum Atropurpureum
8. Juniperus communis depressa Aurea
9. Golden heathers
10. Prunus cyclamina (small tree with pink blossom and coppery foliage)
11. Senecio laxifolius greyii
12. Chamaecyparis lawsoniana Erectus Aurea
13. Rose. Paul's scarlet climber
14. Ceanothus cascade (evergreen)

15. This is a herbaceous border to contain evergreen azaleas and dianthus, and rock roses to trail over brick edges
16. Small bush of Thuja plicata Rogersii
17. This is a terracotta strawberry jar to finish off the end of retaining wall which tapers down to the level of the last step
18. Waterlily
19. Clump of Pontederia cordata

PLAN 11: The knot or herb garden

If you live in or near to London please pay a visit to the Gardens at Hampton Court. Look at the knot garden there—browse in it for a bit so that you get the atmosphere of it. If you are frequent holidaymakers abroad look at some French Potager gardens—even if they belong to a château. Or if you are in search of good food here in England go to Robert Carrier's Hintlesham Hall in Suffolk and look at his charmingly designed kitchen garden. Having made all these visits you can proceed to design your garden without my advice. If however you only have a bicycle I shall have to do my best to describe the sort of garden you are going to make now. Smallness helps here. Also a squarish shape will help and if you are intent on halving a long oblong shape into two squares here is an excellent treatment for one of them.

Let me emphasise here that it need not necessarily be a herb garden. It can be an old-fashioned flower garden (as at Hampton Court), or it can be a very attractive kind of frame in which to grow vegetables.

Ideally your outside hedge should be of Yew. This will give the perfect period effect. You could use beech or cupressus leylandii, or you could be greatly daring and use lattice. On your lattice you could grow espalier fruit trees—apples, pears, plums, peaches, morello cherries, figs.

Looking at design 11 you will see a kind of maze with an outside border which is hedged with lavender. Hidcote might be the best variety for this, as it is compact and very floriferous. Then there is a path. Brick, done in a herringbone pattern would help the period effect. Then you have a centre bed hedged and divided either by low hedge of box or santolina—or to give a colourful effect use both in alternative ways to give a decorative effect. In the centre a topiary figure of Yew—or if you like, a birdbath, or sundial, or even a dove-cote. All would be right for period. If you have trellis fences a pyramid of trellis, rather as they have in Queen Mary's Garden at Regents Park, on which you could grow an old-fashioned rose.

The outside borders will contain the larger plants, be they vegetables, herbs or flower and the middle beds will be planted out with smaller stuff. It is best to keep one bed to each variety and the very centre bed to perhaps have four varieties in well defined clumps.

Round the outside borders you will notice I have dotted specimen trees. Should this be a flower garden there could be flowering shrubs, such as lilac, philadelphus, large shrub roses, magnolias etc.—or even shaped conifers. Should you desire a vegetable garden there could be fruit trees with an occasional space left for a wigwam of bean-sticks for runner beans and peas. Should you be having herbs only, then the two trees by the entrance should be pyramid bay trees or standard bay trees, and the shrubs around should be Rosemary, Southernwood, small Quince trees, groups of Angelica, Globe Artichokes or other tall

B

C

erbs. Siberian Crab apple trees ould look well at each corner (Malus robusta).

Should your choice be vegeables, then each bed should ontain a particular variety, such s lettuce, carrots, beet, parsnips, tc. and rotate at 3 yearly interals the crops with brassicas one ear in a bed and root crops the ext. Parsley makes a good dging plant. The taller vegeables, like Jerusalem Artichokes nd tomatoes, and brussels prouts and peas should be lanted in surrounding borders.

Use your imagination and ecorative flair to have asparagus, ennel, ruby chard, parsley, beetoot and other decorative and olourful vegetables in such uxtaposition as to give as pleasng a general picture as possible.

If you are going to have a lower garden, here is a wonderul place to plant the oldashioned shrub roses—the

Surround to be of white squared trellis with wooden pillars supporting at approximately 5 feet intervals. These to be covered with climbing and rambler roses and clematis. The first border to contain at intervals pyramid fruit trees. With pyramid bay trees either side of the gateway. Hedges— about 1 foot high of either box or santolina to form boundaries of path and beds and borders.

Beds 1–5 and borders to be planted with herbs or vegetables or flowers as explained in text.

larger ones round the outside border—by old-fashioned roses I mean the gallicas, the musk roses, the damasks and the alba roses, moss, Bourbon, species, rugosa, and contrary-like the modern shrub roses (which are new inventions, as it were, on the old themes). The old shrub roses are a most interesting and complicated study on their own and I can best recommend you to read *Shrub Roses of Today* and *Climbing Roses Old and New* by Graham Stuart Thomas and *Shrub Roses for Every Garden* by Michael Gibson. (The species roses by the way are mostly too big for the small garden.) The nursery which specializes in the old-fashioned roses is John Mattocks of Oxford. If you decide on a theme of old-fashioned flowers then a nice idea might be to take a list of flowers mentioned in Shakespeare. There is an informative and poetic book by Roy Genders called *Growing Old Fashioned Flowers* and Vita Sackville-West's books are full of references—she loved old-fashioned flowers. Choose from—Primroses and Polyanthuses, Auriculas, Pinks and Border Carnations, Violets, Pansies and Violas, Bergamots, Bleeding Hearts (Dicentra spectabilis), Christmas Roses, Lychnis, Day Lilies and other Lilies, such as Madonna Lilies, Honeysuckles, Daisies, Foxgloves, Hollyhocks, Daffodils, and Tulips—it might be a good idea to look at some of the old Dutch flower paintings and make a list from them.

For paths you could use Chamomile, Creeping Thyme and Pennyroyal.

PLAN 12: The decorative kitchen garden

No effort is made to split up the garden—one sees the whole as a decorative vegetable plot. The paths can be of gravel, brick, cobbling or stone slabs. I think perhaps I would prefer brick in a herringbone pattern or gravel.

The centre of the formal pattern is a pool in the design with carp in it. You could try a special way of rearing rainbow trout recommended by Thomson & Morgan of Ipswich. On the other hand the whole area could be paved over with a topiary feature in the centre, birdbath or sundial. Indeed, the pool area could be a centre bed and planted with some large feature like Angelica or Bay.

The long borders round the edges of the garden are backed by fruit. There can be cordon apples or espalier or fan-shaped trees of either pear, morello cherry, peach or apricot. Plums too might be attempted. Between these more permanent features lengths of raspberry cane could be planted or loganberries, blackberries (cultivated ones—Himalayan Giant) or Boysenberries.

In season round the borders and spaced at regular intervals you can erect wigwams of beansticks—for beans remember there are white flowered and purple flowered beans as well as the scarlet runner. Wigwams also can be made of peasticks for peas—one could choose one main crop variety, like 'Trio' or 'Gloriosa', or, using earlies and second earlies like 'Feltham First' and 'Onward', one could make a succession.

It might be a nice idea to plant Jerusalem Artichokes in groups at each corner of the plot, together with and growing amongst the annual Sunflower. They are related with similar foliage, and make a bold showing.

Also in the borders in bold clumps positioned according to aspect have Angelica (7 feet), Globe Artichokes (5 feet), Rhubarb; perhaps one clump in the middle of each border.

Then in clumps, sometimes in regimented squares, have sweet corn, leeks, onions, french dwarf beans. The bush tomatoes will look well in groups of three or four and remember the yellow fruited ones. Aubergines look exotic too. In these borders you can also grow Red Lettuce, copper-coloured Fennel, variegated lemon balm, ruby chard, beetroot, red cabbage and variegated kale—all making colourful and unusual plants.

Edge the centre beds with Applemint (the white and green variegated variety), Jackman Rue, Tarragon, Oregano and Nasturtiums (the dwarf Tom Thumb), Alpine Strawberries (Fragaria Baron von Solemacher), Santolina (Cotton Lavender), Chives, Purple Sage

1. Standard Bay trees
2. Groups of Sunflowers and Jerusalem Artichokes alternately
3. Large group of Angelica
4. Large group of Globe Artichokes
5. Large group of Rhubarb
6. Parsley
7. Variegated lemon balm
8. Copper Fennel
9. Red Lettuce in rows
10. Ruby Chard in rows
11. Sweetcorn in squares
12. Leeks in rows
13. Rosemary bushes
14. Beetroot in groups
F. Fruit trees
In Beds A and B Decorative rows of carrots, swedes, parsnips, turnips, lettuce and radishes in successions.
In Beds C and D Cauliflower, Variegated Kale, Cabbage, Savoy and Red Cabbage.
Around the beds borders of:
A. Nasturtiums and Marigolds Alpine Strawberries— Fragaria Baron von Solemacher Santolina Purple Sage Variegated Apple Mint
B. Santolina Purple Thyme Nasturtiums (Tom Thumb) and marigolds Variegated Sage
C. Apple Mint Purple Thyme Rue, tarragon, oregano, chives, Alpine Strawberries
D. Purple Sage, rue, tarragon, oregano Variegated Sage Lemon thyme Chives

urple Thyme, Variegated Sage white, green and pink all on ne leaf!), Parsley, Lemon Thyme and Marigolds.

Inside the four beds, remembering to use them in yearly crop rotation (roots one year, rassicas the next, legumes the ext) make decorative rows of arrots, swedes, parsnips, turnips, radishes. (There is a radish alled Sakurigma Mammoth hich grows to several pounds a root! It is mild, crisp and stores well.) All kinds of lettuces with Webbs Wonderful being decorative, crisp and crinkly! In other beds grow cauliflowers, kale, sprouting broccoli, cabbage, savoys and red cabbage.

A lot depends on your artistry in the lay-out of the vegetables and in keeping them trim with no dead leaves and beans and peas well tied in to preserve the artistic effect.

PLAN 13: A miniature 'forest glade'

A forest glade sixty feet by forty-eight feet is an absurdity. Once we have assured ourselves of this we will now have fun in creating one! All the trees are small, and some are just large shrubs and we will assume that there is a large dark hedge enclosing all and not included in our measurements!

The centre of the garden is a lawn, containing an island bed and around the lawn is an exuberant encroachment of flowering and foliage shrubs and trees which should give you a great deal of colour both in bloom and foliage, and such a terrible time keeping everything within bounds, pruning judiciously here and thinning out carefully there—and in ten years time you will be cursing my ridiculously ambitious frolic and in twenty years time you will have had to move in order to start again.

Anyway let's look at the plan. You leave the house on a suggestion of a few, very old moss grown bricks, inserted into the grass to give a dry area near the house. The placing of them is informal and slightly below the lawn to help mowing the edges. The edges of the beds are serpentine and the inhabitants of the borders are so planted to spill over and camouflage the edges.

The centre bed may make the garden even more crowded and is optional. You could make this an island bed of a few contrasting heathers and tiny conifers. The idea of the bed is to give you a walkaround and so that you do not see all of the garden from the house. The key to the plan describes all.

Ferns are splendid plants for the woodland garden. Amongst them bulbs—snowdrops, scillas, muscaris, leucojums, bluebells and narcissus and daffodils, should be planted liberally.

Other bulbs for massing in the woodland garden are: aconite, anemone, chionodoxa, colchicum, crocus, ixia. Bulbs for groups in the wild garden could be: fritillaria, Gladiolus primulinus, Iris pumila, Lilium chalcedonicum, L. tigrinum 'Splendens', and montbretia. When you plant your bulbs, never put them formally in lines—it is best to shut the dogs in the house and then to throw down a handful in front of you and to plant them as they fall. This way you will get a natural informality.

Plants for the woodland garden: aconitum, lathyrus (the everlasting pea—this will need sun), myosotis, digitalis, lily-of-the-valley, meconopses, orchids, primroses and primulas, violets, polygonatum (Solomon's Seal), various flowering nettles.

1. Pyrus salcifolia pendula
2. A dozen yellow heathers e.g. Erica carnea 'Aurea'
3. Berberis darwinii
3a. Juniperus communis 'Hibernica'
4. Sambucus Nigra Aurea
5. Lonicera nitida 'Baggesons Gold'
6. Floribunda Rose 'Queen Elizabeth' (3 plants)
7. Rhododendron 'Pink Pearl'
8. Elaegnus pungens Maculata
9. Prunus 'Shimidsu Sakura' (Small slow growing white Japanese Cherry)
10. Miscanthus sinensis 'Gracillimus'
11. Ilex altaclarens 'Golden King'
12. Fatsia japonica
13. Buddleia davidii 'Black Knight'
14. Senecio laxifolius
15. Floribunda
16. rose 'Iceberg'
17. Prunus cerasifera Nigra
18. Gleditzia triacanthos 'Sunburst'
19. Several evergreen Azaleas. Choose at yoir garden centre

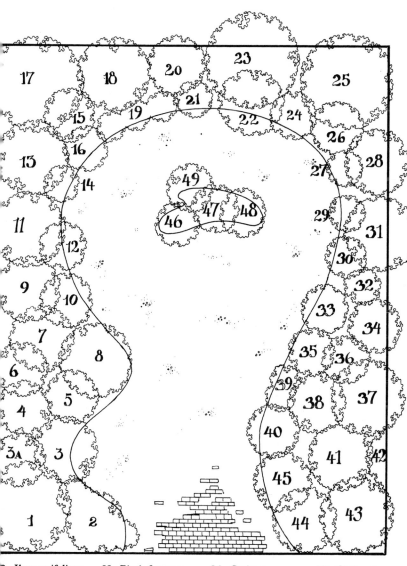

34. Cornus alternifolia 'Argentea'
35. Picea pungens Prostrata
36. Rosa rubrifolia (Cut back hard in spring for best foliage effect)
37. Acer pseudoplatanus Atropurpureum (When big enough grow a Clematis hybrida Sieboldii through this tree)
38. Philadelphus coronarius Aureus
39. Hosta siebodiana Elegans (Clump of several plants)
0. Floribunda Rose 'Iceberg'
41. Azalea mollis
42. Clematis hybrida Sieboldii (See No. 37)
43. Amelanchier laevis
44. Weigela florida Variegata
45. Juniperus virginia 'Greyowl'
46. Salix lanata
47. Spartium junceum (Spanish Broom)
48. Spiraea × arguta
49. Syringa vulgaris 'Mme Lemoine' Get some Maidenhair spleenworts to grow amongst the bricks.

0. Ilex aquifolium Pyramidalis Fructuluteo (Dark green holly with yellow berries)
1. Phlomis fruticosa (Jerusalem sage)
22. Pieris formosa 'Wakehurst'
23. Chamaecyparis lawsoniana 'Stewartii'
25. Chamaecyparis lawsoniana 'Erecta'
26. Cotinus Coggygria 'Royal Purple'
27. Evergreen Azalea 'Blue Danube'
28. Acer 'Negundo'
29. Osmanthus delavayi
30. Cytisus × kewensis
31. Viburnum tinus
32. Hamamelis mollis 'Goldcrest'
33. Santolina

PLAN 14: The 'country' town garden

I designed this particular garden because it is simple, cheap to make, and cheap to maintain. It grows plants in a small space mixing flowers with food and has interesting colour schemes combined with many plants—both ordinary and exotic—of many different textures and flowering periods. It is a garden that can be made by the veriest amateur and yet should give pleasure to a sophisticated plants-man.

Mindful of the economic realities of the day here is a small garden which will grow flowers, fruits, herbs and vegetables, the vegetables and fruit being grown amongst the flowers in an orderly riot. I have endeavoured to accentuate colour in four schemes—and I have varied the textures of foliage and the shapes of plants to give as much possible interest in so small an area. Immediately stepping from the house one is on a terrace made of simulated York Paving. The lawn is surrounded by borders which are roughly in four colour sections:

A. Plants and shrubs of coppery red and blue.

B. Plants and shrubs of white and yellow variegations, and yellow flowers and foliage and silver foliage.

C. Plants and shrubs of mauve and blue.

D. Plants and shrubs of red and yellow.

Use is made of all boundaries of wall and fencing with cordon apples, espalier cherries and plums, loganberries and boysen-berries.

1. Cryptomeria Japonica elegans
2. Juniperus media 'Old Gold'
3. Gleditsia triacanthos 'Sun Burst'
4. Pyrus salcifolia pendula
5. Cotinus coggygria Atropurpurea
6. Juniperus sabina 'Blue Danube'
7. Acer negundo vatiegatum
8. Prunus cerasifera pissardii
9. Espalier peach tree
10. Magnolia gradiflora
11. Loganberry
12. Plum. Victoria
13. Boysen berry
14. Cordon apples
15. Rosemary
16. Morello cherry

Plant, Shrub and Vegetable Areas

A. Rose 'Maigold'
Phormium Tenax Purpureum
Avena Candida
Jackman's Rue
Globe Artichoke 'Vert de Laon'
Aubergine
Sweet Pea, 'Blue Mantle'

Rose 'Little Joey'
Berberis Thunbergi Atropurpurea
Purple Sage
Juniperus × Media Pfitzerana Glauca
Eryngium,
Rudbeckia Rustic, Dwarf
Sweet Pea—Black Prince
Copper Foliage Fennel

B. Variegated Apple Mint
Rose 'Iceberg'
Cytisus Kewensis
Mrs Simkins Pink
Parsley
Philadelphus
Viola 'Landgren's Yellow'
Variegated Lemon Balm
Rose 'Golden Showers'

Hosta fortunei pict
Santolina Neapolitana
Green Mystery Tulips
Weigela florida Variegata
Sambucus nigra aurea (shrub)
Phalaris arundinace Picta
Hosta undulata medio—variegata
Lamium galeobdolon 'Variegatum'

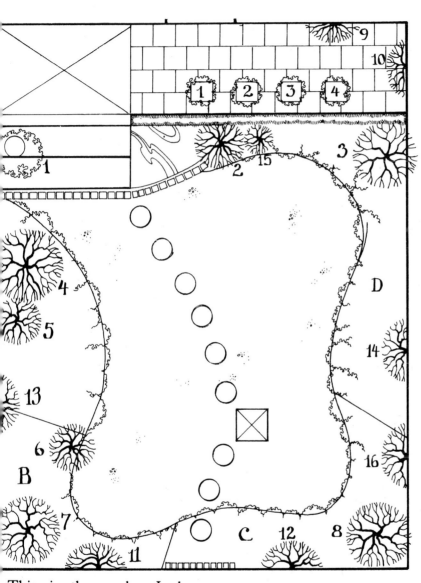

C. Chives
Viola Cornuta
Delphiniums
Thyme
Penstemons,
Various
Fennel

Campanula, Various
Veronica Crater
Lake Blue
Variegated Kale
Acanthus mollis
Rose 'Roseraie de
l'Hay'
Salvia superba 'May
Night'

D. Paeonia
Lupins
Azaleas, Various
Ruby Chard
Geums
Papaver, Various
Pelargonium,
Various
Rose 'Duke of
Windsor'

Marigold, Various
Dianthus
Iris germanica
'Golden Fleece'
Philadelphus
coronarius 'Aureus'
Lobelia Cardinalis
Elaeagnus pungens
Potentilla

This is the garden I de-
gned for Capital Radio at the
helsea Flower Show in the
ummer of 1978 and for which
e Royal Horticultural Society
warded me the Flora Silver
ledal.

PLAN 15: The pond garden

Do you want a garden where you do not have to dig, or mow, or hardly have to weed either? This is it. (Illustrated p. 89.)

I designed this garden for Capital Radio at the 1979 Chelsea Flower Show and was awarded the Banksian Silver Gilt Medal for it.

There is a lot of beauty and plenty to take the eye in the wooden Georgian Chinese panels of the walls, which are spaced between stone pillars; also in the decorative wooden gates and in the white lattice porch over the front door. (This could be a front garden.)

The fences being so decorative are made much of by rambling roses and other wall plants, like Ceanothus and Clematis.

The borders are narrow and edged with stone and contain all kinds of plants, biennial, perennial and annual to exploit various colour schemes and are strengthened at intervals by old-fashioned shrub roses. Roses too grow over the porch and the walls of the house.

As you enter the gates you are immediately standing in a large pond—on ample stepping stones, of course!—made of York paving. This leads up between water and banks of old-fashioned roses and flowers to three steps up to a paved terrace in front of the house. There are beds in front of the house to receive the roots of the climbing plants and roses which will also trail over the lattice porch. On either end of the walls, to give added period flavour, are finials—stone balls and two finely shaped Georgian vases of stone.

The garden is 35 feet long and 26 feet wide and this is a treatment which could be used for a suburban front garden.

In the right hand corner and edge of the pond beneath the terrace are two large Alibaba terra cotta vases, one upright and one which seemingly has fallen down. From the fallen one water pours continuously into the pool. (It is a sort of fountain with an electric pump to ensure the constant flow of water.)

1. Prunus 'Amanogawa'
2. Climbing rose Etoile de Hollande
2a. Espalier Apple Tree
3. Shrub rose Cécile Brunner
4. Spiraea Gold Flame
5. Sweet Corn
6. Azalea hybrid Gibraltar
7. Weigela florida variegata
8, 9, 10, 11. Acer palmatum Dissectum
12, 13, Acer palmatum Atropurpureum
14. Picea pungens Kosta
15. Climbing rose Zephirine Drouhin
16. Shrub rose Frau Dagmar Hastrup
17. Shrub rose Constance Spry
18. Prunus Amanogawa
19. Prunus cerasifera Nigra
20. Ken Muir strawberry pot
21. Spiraea Bridal Wreath
22. Shrub rose Nevada
23. Iris Germanica 'Golden Fleece' and Iris Pallidia
24. Azalea ponticum
25. Perennial candytuft
26. Group of Miniature roses 'Esther's Baby'
27. White pelargoniums
28. Sweet Corn
29. Pink pelargoniums
30. Mauve petunias (Suttons) backed by Shrub rose Roseraie de l'Hay
31. Hebe pinquifolia Pagei
32. Floribunda rose Iceberg
33. Evergreen azalea Hinomayo
34. Pieris Forest Flame
35. Pink evergreen Azalea
36. Dark pink pelargonium Lord Bute in front of Acer palmatum Atropurpureur
37. Copper beech (Fagus sylvatica Purpurea)
38. Rose Canary Bird
39. Several plants of Ageratum mixed with Heliotrope
40. Variegated grass (Gardener's Garters)
41. Stachys lamata
42. Philadelphus coronarius aurea
43. Phormium Tenax
44. Evergreen Azalea Palestrina
45. Chamaecypari pisifera Filifera Aurea
46. Euphorbia wulferii

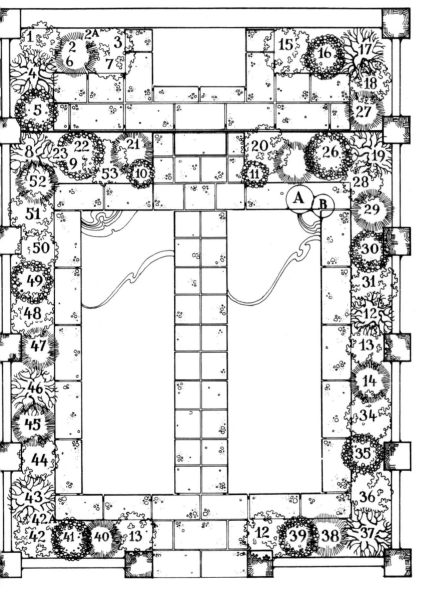

47. Rose Canary
    Bird
48. Hebe
    pinguifolia
    Pagei
49. Cytisus
    scoparius
    Golden
    Sunlight and
    Cytisis ×
    kewensis
50. Rose Gloire de
    Dijon
51. Acer palmatum
52. Rose Blanc
    Double de
    Coubert
53. Clump of
    French
    Marigolds
    (Suttons)

List of plants used
in ponds:
Caltha palustris
Plena (Double
Marsh Marigold)
Mentha aquatica
(water mint)
Arum lilies van
Crowborough
Iris Kaempferi
Variegata
Various water lilies
Water Hyacinth
Chinese water
cabbage

Index

In the text of this book all plant names have been set in the same type face for ease of reading. In the index however you will find the proper botanical name for each plant in *italic type*—as is common practice—and the common or colloquial names in roman type. Both botanical and colloquial names are given and cross-referenced in the index to help you with plant identification. Illustration references are in *italic type*.

Index

Index

127

Index

ACKNOWLEDGEMENTS

Acknowledgements are due to the following for kind permission to reproduce photographs:
Michael Alcott pages 28–9; Cement and Concrete Association page 22; *Evening Standard* page 95; Ferndale page 85; Fox Photos page 25; Mucklow Stone page 21 (lower photograph); Roger Pennington pages 33, 89, 91; Bob Price page 20 (lower photograph); Charles Thewenetti pages 1, 40 (right hand photograph), 49, 56, 57, 68, 69, 76; John Topham Picture Library pages 12, 13, 17, 20–1, 37, 40 (left hand photograph), 41, 45, 48, 49 (right hand photograph), 61, 64–5, 72, 73, 77, 93; Michael Warren pages 9, 80–1. Garden plans drawn by Marilyn Day.

Metric conversion table

inches	cm	feet	cm	yards	metres	sq. yards	sq. metres
1	2.5	1	30	1	0.9	1	0.8
2	5.0	2	60	2	1.8	2	1.6
3	7.5	3	90	3	2.7	3	2.5
4	10.0	3⅓	100	4	3.6	4	3.3
5	12.5			5	4.5	5	4.
6	15.0			6	5.4	6	5.
7	17.5			7	6.4	7	5.
8	20.0			8	7.3	8	6.
9	22.5			9	8.2	9	7.
10	25.0			10	9.1	10	7.
11	27.5						
12	30.0						